The Royal Commonwealth Society.

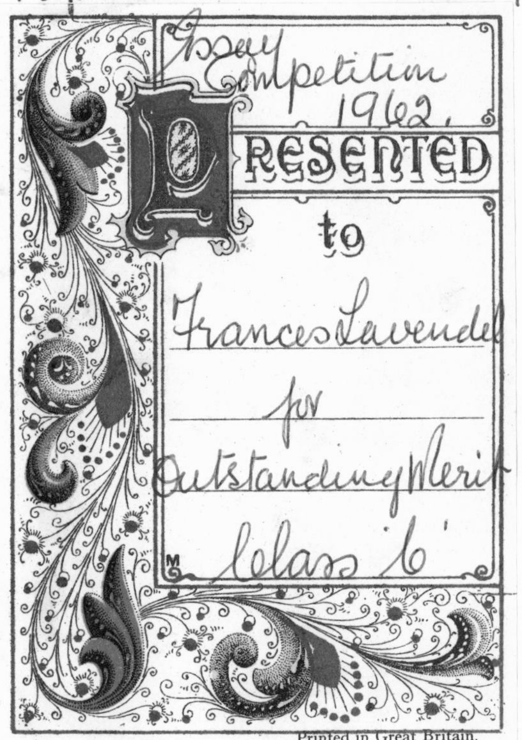
Essay Competition 1962.
PRESENTED
to
Frances Lavendel
for
Outstanding Merit
Class '6'
Printed in Great Britain.

Outdoor rambles

Longmans, Green and Company

TORONTO
NEW YORK
LONDON

Stuart L. Thompson

Outdoor rambles

Illustrated by Geoffrey Goss

Longmans, Green and Company
20 *Cranfield Road, Toronto* 16
Longmans, Green and Co. Inc.
55 *Fifth Ave., New York* 3
Longmans Green and Co. Ltd
6–7 *Clifford Street, London W.*1

First Edition, 1958

Dedicated to my mother,

who was ever sympathetic with her son's outdoor tastes.
"Away you go, laddie. You have your old clothes on so I don't care what you do to them. Have a good time, and you'll be back when you come."
How often have I heard her say those words as I left home for a boyhood ramble?

The rambles

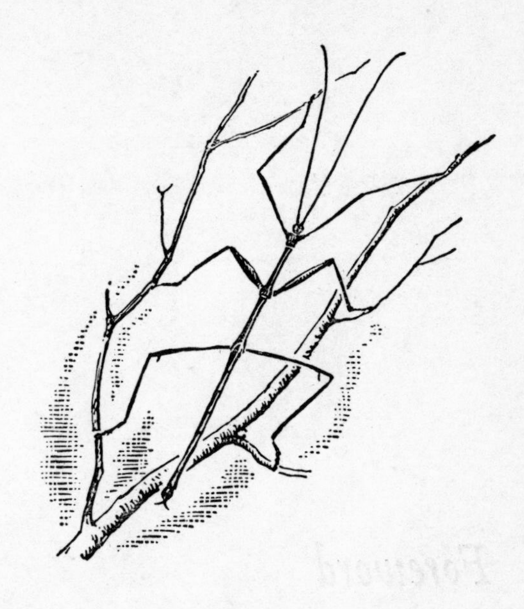

Foreword

"WHY don't you write a book?" How many times have I been asked this by my friends and acquaintances? As though in the mere writing of a book I could tell fully the keen enjoyment we have had together outdoors.

Cold type and even good illustrations can never reproduce actual experiences. But as none of us can relive past pleasures, the next best thing is to recall them in memory and share them in the retelling.

The incidents related in the following pages are all actual experiences I have had during a lifetime of rambling outdoors. As will be seen, some recount times spent with groups on active week-ends covering miles of territory, or on strenuous canoe trips over lake and portage, while others tell of times spent with one or two companions in a few quiet hours afield. Others again tell of what I have seen and enjoyed when alone, often on a dewy morning before the world was awake, during sunny noontide hours, or even when on long lonely tramps at night, sometimes on snow-shoes over the moonlit snow. And still others have come to me quite casually as though Nature herself were saying: "Here's something interesting I want you to see." And in all I have realized:

"There is a pleasure in the pathless woods,
There is a rapture on the lonely shore."

The source of this material has been gleaned in many cases from memory sharpened by keen interest, but largely from some fifty or so years of diaries. The first entries were made on school-books which should have been used for other—though I think not better—purposes. The last entry was made last week when, with three like-minded companions, I spent the morning afield studying the tracks left by the various woodland creatures on the light snow.

All these stories have been reproduced before in some form. For their re-telling here I wish to acknowledge with grateful thanks the kind permission given by the CBC *for the use of many broadcasts given by me in several series over the years; and for the articles, the General Board of Religious Education, the United Church Publishing House, Toronto* Saturday Night, Canadian Forest and Outdoors, Canadian Red Cross Junior, *and the* Totem Board.

Though not told in their original form, the various stories have been arranged so that the experiences and incidents blend one into another, more or less seasonally, to make what is hoped will be an interesting whole.

STUART L. THOMPSON *Toronto February* 1958.

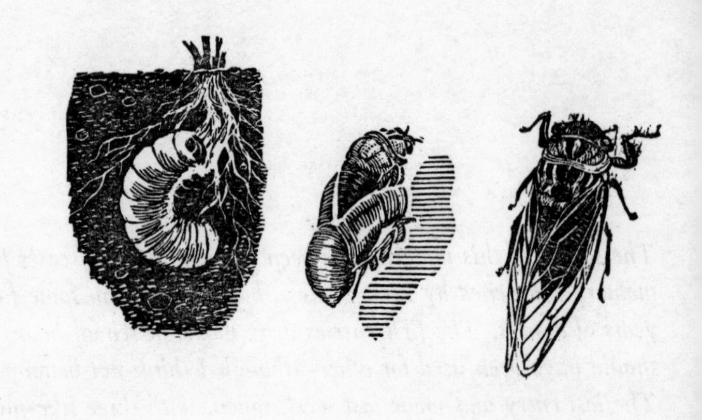

Outdoor rambles

A week-end really outdoors

Did you ever spend a week-end outdoors? Not at your summer cottage, or in a tent, but really outdoors—surrounded by nature everywhere and with the sky overhead. We had that experience one spring and I must tell you of all we saw.

There were nine of us, two who drove the cars and all the rest schoolboys. But regardless of age every one was keenly interested in nature lore. We took our notebooks and field-glasses and one or two brought cameras. We wore old clothes and got away right after lunch on a bright Saturday.

Our destination was to be a rough section of the county some two hours' ride from the city. Now a two-hour ride will take you a long way, if you go fast enough. But we drove at what is called "ornithological speed"—that is a speed at which we could stop quickly if any of us saw anything interesting on the way, for example, a shrike on a post, a hawk flying overhead, or a promising bit of woodland to examine. Once or twice we got out and rambled about for a few minutes. There was no hurry.

We had hours of daylight ahead of us, and we did not want to spoil the trip by going into the ditch or having a wreck on the way.

At length we arrived at the place we had in mind. It was a wide stretch of hilly country, dotted with woods here and there and broken by rough clearings with their stumps and boulders. In one place there was a large swamp. Altogether it was a very promising spot for all kinds of nature study. Now I would not have you shrink from the thoughts of a swamp. No naturalist neglects a swamp. He considers it one of nature's gifts to mankind. Such a spot is sure to be full of all types of wild life, both animal and floral, much of it to be found nowhere else.

As soon as we got things settled in camp, which was an open grassy spot with its stumps and rocks in a bit of woodland, we struck out for the nearby hill. After an interesting half-hour's walk and climb we were looking out over as fine a view as one could wish to see. Below us stretched miles and miles of open country with its woods and clearings as far as the distant horizon. Much of this landscape was occupied by the swamp mentioned, which promised so much. Here and there through the trees we could see the gleaming curves of the river as it wound its way through the swamp. And leading up the hill lay the long thin ribbon of roadway by which we had come, seeming to be the only way into this lonely land. Over all this the setting sun was casting his long rays aslant, bringing out the soft greens of the nearby forest and the blues of the dim distance in full billowy mounds. What a prospect for our ramble of to-morrow!

After a cheery supper around the camp-fire, we strolled down the road to a scrubby bit of meadow which seemed a good woodcock place, and settled ourselves to wait until this strange bird began his weird music. For some time we remained very still, talking in low tones, for the woodcock is shy and might be hiding but a few paces away. At last on the still evening air there sounded a peculiar buzzing nasal note, "Pe-ent," it is written in books, but in cold type this gives no suggestion of its misleading quality. Was the sound coming from a few feet away or many yards? Suddenly one of the party said, "There he goes, now watch."

Then came the clear whistling sound of rapidly moving wings, and from the nearby thicket, showing sharply against the glowing western sky, sprang a bird. Around and around he flew in a wide circle, mounting higher and higher. Up, up he went, one hundred, two hundred feet or more, the whistling sounding sharper and sharper as he went. Then, as he paused, the whistling ceased and he poised a moment uttering a low mellow twittering call. Several times this was repeated and down again to earth came the performing musician in long graceful sweeping curves to settle in his thicket-home. Silence reigned for some time. Then again we heard the nasal "Pe-ent," the prelude to another sky-dance aloft.

We lingered as long as daylight permitted watching the sky-dance of the woodcock and then struck out for camp. It had been a delightful experience. We felt as though we had been peeping through the curtain of twilight, and had seen one of nature's secrets which few were privileged to learn—a shy, secretive bird indulging in his love-manoeuvres.

That night we slept out.

Have you ever slept out? Not on the veranda, but really out on the ground under the stars? That is what each of us did that night. Gathering leaves and evergreen boughs, each one made himself comfortable for the night.

We humans are very much inclined to think of night as that long, dark, silent time when there is little astir and nothing happening. But, if we only have ears to hear, what we can learn of all that goes on in nature's world during these hours of darkness! That night as we lay surrounded on all sides by nature, wrapped in gloom and with the sky overhead sparkling with stars, we heard many voices and many sounds seldom heard during the hours of daylight. Far away across the swamp the great-horned owl was hooting in deep bass notes. And, as though in contrast, quite nearby came the sweet liquid trill of the screech owl. In our own woods close by a ruffed grouse was drumming at intervals through the night. From the ponds near the swamp the hylas—those pigmies of frogland—were piping in notes so shrill and vibrant that we wondered how such tiny throats could send music so far. Mingled with their voices came the long resonant trill of the common toad. But above all these, from near and far, we heard the oft-repeated chant of the many whippoorwills as they answered each other with almost monotonous frequency. All voices of the night these; and yet occasionally a daytime singer, a song sparrow or a white-throat, sang dreamily as though in sleep.

We were all up before sunrise. In a twinkling the silent camp became a chatter of voices as each told of what he had heard during the night, of how he had slept—or hadn't slept. Soon the fire was going, fresh water brought from the nearby stream, and in a short time we all sat down to a good outdoor breakfast of oatmeal, bacon, toast and coffee. This was to be a great day. Before the sun was above the tree-tops breakfast was finished, camp tidied up and all ready to start out on our morning hike.

There is no time like early morning for seeing birds. It is then they are most active and sing at their fullest and best. Even as we ate breakfast we heard on all sides, from the woods, the clearing, and the swampy thicket, a wonderful chorus of bird song, full, free and of infinite variety. The familiar robin was here just as we heard him in the city. A curious oriole came when we called him and he answered us from the nearby tree-top. A modest chipping sparrow was trilling from the bush close at hand. From the woods came the whistle of the white-throat and the cooing of the mourning dove. The hymn of the hermit thrush mingled with the strains of the veery and the olive-backed thrushes. From the clearing we heard the clear whistle of the meadowlark and the notes of the vesper sparrow. In fact we might have stayed here all day and found bird life aplenty, but we felt the urge to go for a hike.

Our route led us first through some rough country where the road was almost obscured with bush, across a bridge over a pure woodland brook. Had we been on a fishing trip I would call it a trout stream. Then out on to the open country which we crossed and came to a high bluff overlooking miles of wooded swampland. All this way we had heard and seen bird life. Now, with this vista, we were in the best position to see everything. We could watch all that flew across the sky and look down at many birds in the tree-tops. In this advantageous position we lingered for a long time searching the scenery before us with our field-glasses, calling out anything that came into view or new discoveries as any of us saw them.

It was great fun, for example, to hear the notes of the scarlet tanager, the rose-breasted grosbeak, or the purple finch, then see who could find it first. But there were many songs we heard without the bird being in sight. It was interesting then to sort out, as it were, this song from that in the general chorus all about us. Such sorting required discriminating ears.

All was good training for the eyes, too. For sometimes there were silent birds out in that sea of foliage which we had to watch closely for distinctive markings, a gleam of colour, or a characteristic pose or movement which would reveal the owner's name. A marsh hawk flew by in the distance. We knew him at once by his long tail and white spot. Then a great blue heron crossed our vision. His slow flagging flight with long legs streaming behind marked him. We noticed that several herons flew to a certain spot in the swamp. This meant a colony of these birds nesting there. On another occasion later several of us visited this "heronry" as a nesting colony is called.

Nor were our observations confined to bird life. A fat woodchuck was dozing on a stump half a mile away. Little did he dream that nine pairs of eyes were watching him as he basked. Yet I feel sure that the nimble little red squirrel nibbling buds on the limb below us knew full well that he was being watched.

But we wanted to learn what was in that swamp. It was not far away and before long we were in its depths. Everywhere was a dense tangle of purple dogwood, yellow willow, grey alder and other bushes, with tall cedars, spruces, hemlocks and balsams mixed with elms, ashes and maples overhead. The ground was comfortably dry so that we could walk about easily. Here and there were pretty little streams strickling along, losing themselves amid the fallen logs and foliage of the forest. So primeval and unspoilt was it all that we could easily imagine we were the first ever to visit that spot. At some time long ago huge trees had fallen and now lay as great moss-covered logs, some with smaller trees growing out of their ruins. Perhaps these giants had lain thus prostrate for half a century or longer. Others again showed signs of having been blown down during the recent wind-storm and were only beginning the long process which eventually changes sound wood into the soil of the forest floor.

Everywhere we found wild flowers. The dainty mitrewort; the violets, blue, white and yellow; squirrel's corn and Dutchman's breeches—those twins of the forest so often confused; patches of red and white trilliums; the oddly shaped jack-in-the-pulpit; the modest little star flower; and the well-named goldthread with its yellow wire-like roots. All these we found in prodigal abundance.

But more than birds and flowers interested these boys! Soon all were engaged in the fascinating pastime of what might be called a woodland treasure hunt. This is really nothing more than rolling over logs and ripping open old stumps. For there is no

guessing what one may discover in doing this. Under a damp log a salamander may come to light. He is a limp smooth-skinned little creature, like a diminutive alligator, and if you are not quick he will wriggle out of sight, back into the rotten wood. The next log may hide a mouse's nest. Away scampers the owner, soon to be lost amid the trash of the forest. Or it may be a jumping mouse which vanishes in long bounds like a tiny kangaroo. Anything may come to light on a woodland treasure hunt.

But there is one little animal we discovered that day which I must tell you of especially. He was not under a log but hiding for the day in an old woodpecker's hole. We expected him to be there so we tapped the tree. At once he looked out at us, just as one would look out of the upstairs window to see who is at the door. Then he came right out and ran up the tree-trunk, sprang into the air and floated gently downward in a long graceful curve, alighting in the daintiest way on the trunk of the nearby tree. Now you have guessed his name—the flying squirrel.

Few people ever see this little acrobat of the night. All day long he dozes in some snug retreat. His long whiskers, big ears and large gentle eyes all tell us his nocturnal habits. How does he fly? you ask. He doesn't. All he does is stretch his four feet far apart, making himself as flat as possible, spring into the air and float away down in a long sloping skim to the next tree, helped greatly by his long flat tail.

Well, we had a great trip. When the time came to return home we counted up and found we had seen over sixty different kinds of birds, numerous other woodland creatures and countless wild flowers. Some of the boys had taken pictures with their cameras, others had made sketches in their notebooks, and all of us had enjoyed ourselves for a whole thirty-six hours surrounded by nature.

How much did the trip cost us? Well, it was just about the cheapest holiday you could imagine. But had we all been millionaires we could not have had a happier time, for there are some things which money cannot buy.

Eyes and no eyes

March music

Coltsfoots

Jack-in-the-pulpits

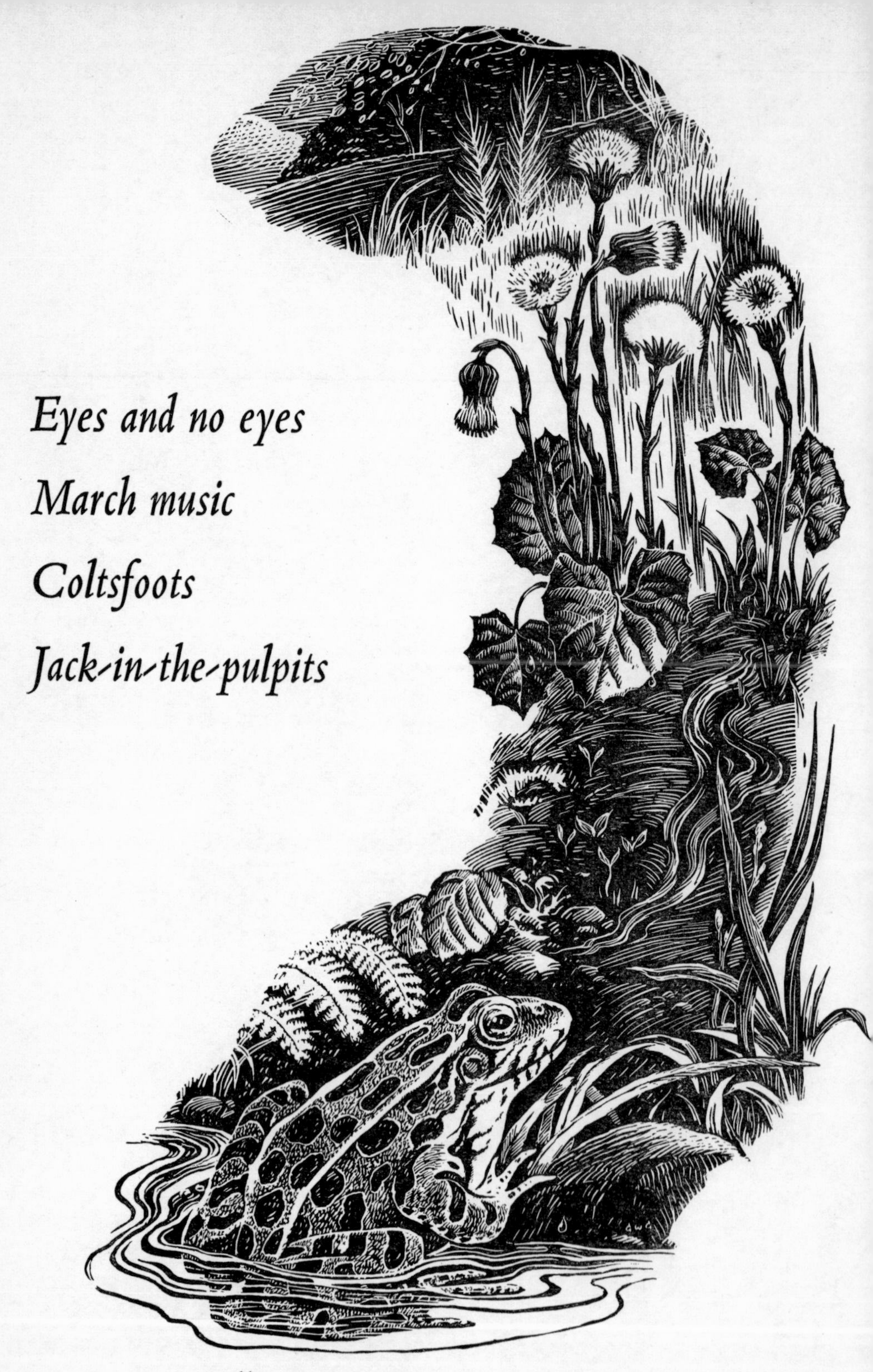

Ramble two

ON MARCH 15th, 1902, in Toronto, two of us boys started out on one of our Saturday rambles. We were keen to learn birds and this day we were out to make a record. Our route lay through Rosedale Ravine, where the road wound for a mile or so flanked by high wooded hills, then opened up into the Don Valley. We followed this valley a couple of miles or so, then entered the smaller valley of Mud Creek, and continued along the elevated path that marked the right-of-way of the former belt-line railway. After many curves this led us out onto the fields to the north of the city. These we crossed and finally arrived home, tired, hungry and muddy but very happy.

In our boyish way we felt we had done something that day. Our long tramp had not been for nothing. We had noted seven species of birds. Never before had we made such a record. Some were common—that is, we had seen several of each—but of others we had found only one or two individuals. That day marked an epoch in our bird studies. Now, as I look back on it in the light of all the more productive days that have filled the years since, there is something amusing about a long tramp on a fine spring day, through splendid country, producing only seven species of birds and, all told, not a great many individuals.

One spring, years later, I resolved to travel the same ground (or as nearly as the growing city would permit) and see how many more birds I could find than on that memorable day of twenty-five years previous. It was characteristic of a later time in life that owing to the pressure of business, I found it impossible to try my experiment on exactly the same date. We cannot always enjoy the freedom of youth. Accordingly it was March 20th—not 15th—when I set out. The weather was the worst possible for such a venture. It was dull and cold, with a strong east wind and flying clouds of snow. At about the same time in the morning as before, I entered the Rosedale Ravine. Almost at once I heard, then saw, several crows overhead. Then, as I peered through the bars of a nearby fence, I saw a fine robin, which was singing in a far-away voice the muffled song sometimes heard. Not far from him was a black squirrel. Such a sight would have been a marvel twenty-five years ago. There were practically no black squirrels about the city's outskirts then. Today they are commonly seen on the streets. Here, too, I found a red squirrel nibbling on the frozen apples of a solitary tree.

And all this before I had gone fifty yards in the ravine!

It was a very uninviting woodland that sloped down on both sides towards the central road. But, as I have long since learned that effort brings its reward, I spent some time scrambling about the snowy hillside. Before long I came upon a song sparrow in the low bushes. Here was a bird of whose presence I should never have learned from the road below for he was quite silent.

At length I came to the spot known as Castle Frank. Local history tells us that on the hilltop here, Governor Simcoe built a woodland residence, naming it after his son Frank. I followed the ancient roadway up its winding ascent. It was old when we first walked up it, now the trickling freshets of twenty-five more springs have worn its surface into tiny canyons and the then slender trees are stouter and arch it over thickly. When I reached the top of the hill I became exposed to the full force of the eastern gale as it swept across the valley and up the almost bare hillside. What a dreary scene that valley was! There was not a bright spot of colour in it to relieve the drab vista of flying snow. Yet here, amid the storm, I caught the notes of a junco, though I failed to find the bird.

As my route lay up the valley I felt my way cautiously down the slippery hillside to the level ground below and turned northward. At an old landmark we call "Sugarloaf Hill" I found a little flock of bluebirds keeping out of the storm. As I watched them a flock of grackles flew over "clicking" in their harsh way. A little farther up the valley I came upon one of those eyesores sometimes found near a large city—a garbage dump. Today the kindly snow was covering the worst of it. Yet strange to say this malodorous blotch on the face of nature brought about greatly improved bird conditions. Here were hundreds of gulls who had learned that this spot provides fodder. I approached cautiously and studied the assembly through my field-glasses. It was a pretty sight. Before me stood acres of stately gulls of two species, the herring and the ring-billed. They were in all stages of plumage, from the mottled slate-grey of the immature, to the pure white and pearly blue of the adult. Some were standing still, soberly facing the wind; others were tearing at the refuse. Amongst them walking here and there were many grackles and a few crows. Was there ever such a contrast in plumages? The immaculate gulls were difficult to see against the snowy background, which at the same time conspicuously showed up jet-black grackles and crows. One could almost imagine the gulls were standing aloof and dignified in their camouflage, while the black rascals felt visible and betrayed by nature.

Leaving the dump and following the river, I came upon a broad beach of gravel. Not a cheery spot, with much dark, muddy water; and yet two killdeer plover sprang up and flew off crying in alarm at my approach. Near here, too, I found a little isolated clump of willows where some tree sparrows were twittering their contentment, and by the merest chance I caught sight of a solitary brown creeper dodging about the tree trunks.

And now comes the strange irony of the trip. Amid such uninviting places as snowy open valleys, garbage dumps and isolated groves of trees I had found abundant life. But when my way led me, as it had years ago, up the quiet winding valley of Mud Creek, snug and sheltered from the wind and overgrown with mixed woods, I neither saw nor heard a single bird for over a mile, then found only three silent bluebirds and two juncos.

However, as I passed a certain park-like spot, recollection moved me to look into the white oaks near at hand. I half expected to see, as we had once seen, a flock of strange birds in the branches. The familiar locality had vividly recalled that past experience. Had we known it, the strange birds on that occasion were purple finches, but they remained a puzzle for many a day after. No such birds were here today. There were even fewer trees, for the park-like spot had been "improved" and now appeared as a flourishing cemetery, with more white grave-stones than white oaks. This is quite in keeping with the times, of course, for if cities will increase and people will live *all* their lives in cities, it follows that city cemeteries must increase also. However, my purple finches were not here to-day so I walked on.

The valley opened up onto the fields shortly and again I came to a refuse pile, where nine herring gulls and two crows were foraging. At this point, true to my route of long ago, I must cross the fields. From the very first weed-patch I flushed two starlings. Here indeed was a new bird. We should never have seen him twenty-five years ago. Song sparrow, bluebird, junco and killdeer, all were here then. It would have needed only observation to find them, but no amount of observation or enthusiasm would have revealed the starling. He is a later introduction into this country, and just wasn't here to see twenty-five years ago.

The open fields brought me into the storm again. The wind swept over them unobstructed, yet amid it I caught the clear whistle of the meadow lark. The sound came from far away over the fields where I could see fertilizer had been spread about. This meant food for birds and they had come to it so freely that in a fair-sized area I counted ten meadow larks, nine starlings, two crows and two killdeer all foraging about. In all these fields on our former tramp we had found but one species of bird—the horned lark.

I was nearing home now. I had a feeling that I had done well, and could enjoy a good dinner. After many snowy acres of wind-swept fields, I entered a wooded hillside thickly set with thorn bushes. Here the force of the wind was stayed and comparative stillness reigned. As I drew near I heard strange notes—sometimes a clear whistling warble, then an odd chuckle, a rasping screech or a harsh twitter came in turn from the thickets. There was something in the whole comical performance, along with the bleak landscape, that suggested the singer's name—the northern shrike. This bird might be said to be the only singer of the day. It would seem as though the dreary landscape of flying snow made him of the great lone northland feel at home in a way the new arrivals from the south could not feel. He was thriving here, for, as I watched him, he flew to a certain bush and there resumed his meal of a half-eaten mouse spitted on a thorn.

This same thicket held one more secret. As I left the shrike, a large brown bird rose on whistling wings and flew in a wide circle through the woods. I marked the spot and found him not far off. As I expected it was a woodcock. What strange neighbours they made—a shrike and a woodcock in the same thicket! Even their colours were incongruous, the cold blue-grey and the warm brown. I could well imagine the silent woodcock standing disconsolately amid the ever-deepening snow, hearing as he certainly must have heard, the notes of the garrulous shrike, and reflecting to himself, that one might well sing amid a snow-storm when there were fat meadow-mice to find, but how was he, a woodcock, to manage without soft earth and earthworms?

The woodcock was my last observation for the day. Five minutes later I was home. After dinner I got out an old school-book used as a journal and read again the account of March 15th in that bygone year—the proud record of seven species of birds seen. How pitifully it compared with the list of to-day. It could be written thus:

March 15th, 1902—fine spring day; seven species of birds seen; several individuals.

March 20th, 1927—miserable day; fifteen species of birds seen; hundreds of individuals and two squirrels.

Not long ago I told the story of these two days' tramps to a well-known naturalist. Perhaps his laconic comment goes a long way in explanation of the comparison. "Eyes and no eyes," he said briefly.

But not all the music of spring days is made by our feathered songsters. Nature has a chorus of humbler singers, often heard but seldom seen. As the snows of winter melt, forming ponds in the valleys and hollows, a host of tiny creatures is stirred to life in the warm spring air and sunshine; and like our birds they feel they must sing. Who are they? The "spring peepers." Their music is the piping and trilling we all have heard in the spring ponds. But though their notes would be sadly missed were they to be silenced, few people have seen these lowly musicians.

There are several kinds of "spring peepers"—or frogs, for they are really frogs—in this chorus. But I believe the two smallest are the most common and I think the noisiest. One of these is the swamp tree frog and the other Pickering's hyla. When full-grown and in all their noisy glory either is barely one inch long. And yet these diminutive musicians can send forth such penetrating notes that they can be heard half a mile away. And when they all pipe in unison the very air seems to vibrate. And yet when you search for these little pipers to see them perform you find yourself completely baffled. They won't be watched if they know it. The moment a movement appears on the skyline of their pond, the air which was throbbing with voices becomes a blank silence. You may as well leave the pond for no amount of search will reveal a piper.

Would you learn their secret? There are two ways in which you may catch these shy little musicians at their music. One is by locating a pond in full chorus and walking leisurely up to it in plain view. Of course the music ceases the moment you come in sight. Now choose a comfortable spot overlooking the water and sit down and wait—and wait—and wait.

This will be a test of your patience. You wait ten minutes, perhaps fifteen, even twenty. Then, when you are just ready to give up, you hear a single note—just one, like a scout voice sent out to try out the enemy. This scout pipes a few times shyly, then is joined by another and another. In a short time all have forgotten their alarm and again the pond is throbbing with their music.

But your success is only half won. You have yet to see the singer. Remember, you must not move. Keeping in the same position, scan the surface of the pond, especially near the reeds. At last you will be rewarded by seeing, not a frog, but a tiny throat blown up like a balloon. It is the movement of this as the tiny creature pipes that will catch your eye, and next minute you see the piper himself. He is a drab little morsel of life not much bigger than his own balloon-throat. The marvel is that such a wee mite can send forth such a far-reaching voice.

Another way of catching the musicians at it is to approach the pond by easy stages, crouching and creeping, foot by foot, always taking care to keep out of sight. Finally you will arrive at the edge of the pond. Then cautiously, very cautiously, peep over the edge until you have a clear view of its surface and look—again not for frogs, but for the little balloons moving with music. Now, if you must see and examine one of the singers closely, there is nothing else for it but to appear in full sight (silence follows at once of course) and wade right into the water, keeping your chosen marked singer in full view, walk up to his spot and find him.

It is interesting to know that though these little frogs look very much alike and often live and sing together in the same pond, their notes are very different. The swamp tree frog's note is a hard shrill rattle on the ascending scale. It is not pleasing, but has a very penetrating quality. On clear still spring days it can be heard many hundred yards away. The note of Pickering's hyla is a smooth, clear, musical whistle, which like that of his companion can be heard long distances from the singer's home pond. Even the dullest of human ears can detect the difference in these two tiny voices from afar. But of all the tests we can set ourselves, this of discovering, seeing and actually catching one of these humble, inconspicuous, elusive, yet noisy little musicians is the most trying.

Some warm spring day as you wander along the edge of the bank of a stream, you may be surprised to see (if you have eyes!) far below you on the wet, oozy clay a host of bright yellow flowers. As each little bloom gleams out in the spring sunshine against the drab sodden background your first thought is—dandelions already! No, these little golden flowers are not dandelions but coltsfoots. (One would think the plural would be "coltsfeet", but no.) It is now only April, but already the hardy plants are in full bloom. Weeks will elapse before your friend the dandelion will adorn the fields. Yet one can hardly be blamed for mistaking these two flowers. They certainly resemble one another closely. Both are the same bright golden-yellow, and in each case the flower consists of a head of florets on a single stalk. This fact speaks volumes to the botanist. It means they belong to that great family of plants known as *Compositae* or composite flowers. If we examine either the dandelion or the coltsfoot we will find that each tiny yellow floret is in itself a complete flower, which will in time develop into a seed. In both plants the seeds are provided with a little silky parachute which bears the seeds away on the breeze to grow elsewhere. With all these similarities it is no wonder you thought the coltsfoots on the muddy bank were dandelions.

But like most things in nature which appear alike at first, the more closely they are examined, the more they differ. We all know the smooth stem of the dandelion. Often as children we have held it to our lips and by blowing through it made a note like a pipe-organ. You won't do this with the stem of the coltsfoot. It is not hollow and, far from being smooth, is covered with webby hairs and beset with little tags which are really tiny leaves.

Everyone knows the peculiar shape of the dandelion's leaf. In fact it is the sharp jagged points which have given the plant its name, *dent de lion* as the French call it, or "tooth of the lion." And certainly it does suggest a lion's mouth set in a ferocious snarl. Would that all our wild flowers were as aptly named!

Now let us compare this with the leaf of the coltsfoot. But, where is it? Here is the flower in full bloom and yet we see no leaf. You must wait until later in the season. Not until after the pretty yellow flower-heads have bloomed and gone to seed do we find the fully developed leaves of the plant. They are large and broad with pointed angles, bright green above, white with downy cobweb-like appearance beneath. Remember the spot where you found the flowers and search there during the summer, and you will find a crop of leaves instead of flowers.

The coltsfoot is a useful plant. In pioneer days of our country it was considered a good medicine for coughs and colds. Blooming as it did in early spring when the changeable weather was so conducive to such ailments, coltsfoot seemed to offer itself to suffering humanity. Tea brewed from the plant became a home-made remedy. Perhaps it is owing to this that the humble herb has found its way into the modern drug store. Sometimes when you are in the drug store asking for a cough medicine, you may see the clerk get your purchase from a nearby shelf in a box marked "Tussis" among all the strange names that appear there. This word means cough. But what has this to do with our flower the coltsfoot? I turn up my botany for the answer and there find that the scientific name for the coltsfoot is "Tussilago—from the Latin *tussi*, *tussis* a cough, for which the plant is a reputed remedy."

But why then, you ask, should this pretty little yellow flower be named coltsfoot? Well, that I can't tell you. It is like many another name given our wild flowers—imaginative and puzzling. On the other hand, take jack-in-the-pulpit—a strange name for a plant, surely? Yet at a glance we see how apt a name. Here is the pulpit, a high, round, vase-shaped affair over-arched by a graceful curving canopy. Inside stands Jack, bolt upright as a preacher in his pulpit. High above both, on two stems, are spread six leaves, suggesting the airy vaulted ceiling of a great cathedral. So, after all, jack-in-the-pulpit is not such a strange name. In fact many of our wild flowers seem strangely named until we examine them with a little imagination.

Look for Jack towards the end of May, when spring has been safely ushered in, and the time for flowers is with us. At first we may not see him. Though odd in shape he has no brilliant colours. His brightest markings are the long lines of deep purple on the inside of his pulpit. Jack himself wears a purple robe. All else is green or greenish. In his stiff, erect manner he holds forth for several days. Then his long harangue begins to tell on him. Gradually he wilts and leans forward wearily upon his pulpit, then finally droops and falls.

Jack's work is to send out into the world of woodlands around him other preachers like himself to carry on during the next year. But it is only when he dies that the next generation can come to life. After both he and his pulpit are gone, there appears a green lumpy mass in a heap where he was standing. In a few days this mass becomes a brilliant scarlet body of two or three dozen compartments each containing a seed. If all goes well every seed will next year become a preacher in a pulpit in a leafy-arched cathedral of his own.

But for all his benign calling, Jack has a baleful secret in his life. We sometimes hear of the root of all evil; Jack's root is *all* evil! Down under ground, below the plant, is a crooked little bulb. It looks innocent enough, but I believe it is the vilest-tasting thing in all the woods. Never let anyone who may be with you on a woodland ramble tempt you to taste this harmless-looking juicy root. At first it is cool and insipid, but, in a minute or so, the tongue feels a terrible burning sensation as though pricked by a host of tiny needles. Once you have tasted, you must suffer for several minutes. It is too late to retreat. Even a cool drink from the nearby spring will not ease your sufferings.

But the strange thing about the root is that it may be boiled, mashed up and eaten freely. It then tastes rather like turnips. So it is not surprising to learn that Jack's other name is "Indian turnip." Perhaps the Indians ate this root in the early days, but I venture to say that there were many smarting, sore tongues before these children of the forest learned to eat Indian turnip with pleasure!

A canoe trip in spring

Skunk cabbage

Wilson's snipe

In 1635 one of the greatest pioneers, Samuel de Champlain, died at Quebec. What a life he had! He was the son and the grandson of sea captains. Very early in life he crossed the Atlantic when crossing was indeed a journey. He visited many parts of the West Indies and even travelled far inland to Mexico City. Then, after returning to France, he came out to New England some years later and sailed up the St. Lawrence to begin his wonderful career in New France. For years he laboured, directing the colony, building forts, trading with the friendly Indians, fighting the hostile ones and ever exerting his efforts to extend the domain of the king of France. He spent much of his time in exploring new territory, pushing his way far up the mighty Ottawa, then down into what is now New York State, to the historic lake which now bears his name. Again and again he crossed the Atlantic to confer with his royal master and mingle with the life of the court. Finally he returned to New France, where we have reason to believe his real interest lay, to plan and toil as governor of the young colony.

But I believe there is no phase of this wonderful career which appeals to the boy of to-day or grips his imagination so much as those long trips by canoe which Champlain made far inland. Think of paddling on and on, day after day, beyond the farthest outposts of civilization, crossing uncharted lakes, pushing up unknown rivers, with Indian companions, where the white man had never been, where all was rock, river and forest as the Creator had made them, with wild life everywhere and fish and game in abundance. What boy would not be thrilled to go on such trips?

One spring I was fortunate enough to enjoy, though in a lesser degree, this experience which Champlain had so often. Not a long romantic voyage of discovery through unspoilt wilderness with savage companions—I was born three hundred years too late for that! Instead it was my humble lot to have a short, simple canoe trip of a couple of hundred miles in the limited time a city man can snatch from business and call a vacation.

Late summer is the most popular time for canoe trips, for several reasons. The weather is settled usually, the water warm enough for swimming, and greatest of all boons, the scourge of insect pests is passed. But there is such a thing as taking one's vacation so often at the same time of year that, having the same weather, seeing the same scenery and wild life, it becomes monotonous. A trip at another season, therefore, brings a refreshing change.

So, after many canoe trips in summer, this particular year we chose to go during the month of May. How different we found everything! It was like beginning my canoe-trip days all over again. True, the lakes and rivers, the rocks and forest were all as we had always known them, But the fauna and flora were vastly different. Heretofore we had enjoyed the rich maturity of summer; now all the glory of the northern spring was ours to revel in. On all sides we found nature bursting into life anew.

When we began our trip the trees, with the exception of the evergreens, were bare and leafless. But on every twig the buds were swelling and ready to burst into leaf. Whole hillsides of forest were masses of dim colours—the grey of the maples, the pale brown of the birches and aspens, and the light yellow of the willows. Yet over all was the faintest tinge of green. Day after day this hue grew richer and more pronounced, until by the time our vacation had ended the whole landscape was in full leaf, showing the varying shades of green we all knew so well in the forests of former trips.

The forest floor was beautifully carpeted with wild flowers everywhere. Spring beauties covered the ground with masses of purple. Yellow adder's tongues abounded. Squirrel's corn and Dutchman's breeches—two plants so much alike—grew together in broad patches. Violets, white, purple, blue and yellow, were to be seen on all sides. Wild ginger with its half-hidden flower, the white-blossomed hobblebush and the curiously shaped jack-in-the-pulpit were all abundant. And most glorious of all, the trilliums—the large white, the dainty painted, the rich red trillium, all these bloomed everywhere.

There is one plant which I shall always associate with my canoe trips through the north. This is the dainty bunchberry or cornel. It is lowly in growth and has a humble flower of dull white. Others far more attractive may flourish near by, but the bunchberry crowds itself right up to the edge of the trail. As the camper, bowed beneath the upturned canoe, toils over the portage he may not see the trilliums and other beauties scattered through the forest, but his mocassined feet are ever among the bunchberry plants with their four-pointed flowers.

You would never gather the bunchberry for the sake of its flowers. These have little or no colour. When in bloom the plant spreads out to the sunshine four broad pointed bracts of dull opaque white, in the form of a cross. In the centre of this there is a group of tiny florets. When we look at these closely, we find that each of the florets is in itself a perfect flower with all the parts of larger flowers. But they are so small and inconspicuous that we almost overlook them. And what is the broad white cross? This is what often misleads even flower-lovers. Though having the appearance of a flower, these four parts are merely bracts—a sort of coloured leaf. Their duty is to gleam in the sunshine, thereby tempting the wandering bee to alight and scramble about for nectar, stirring up the pollen to fertilize the tiny florets.

Nature does not keep things which have become useless. And so, as soon as the florets are fertilized, the bracts wilt and drop away. Their work was done when they attracted the bee. Now the flowers develop in earnest. Soon the unripe fruit appears and grows, until by midsummer the humble little plant has changed its colour-scheme. Earlier in the season it was green and white—not a very strong or pleasing combination. But now as they ripen the berries take on the most vivid of scarlets. What a riot of colour! What a striking and yet harmonious contrast of hues! The gorgeous scarlet is even more intensified by its background of green leaves. No wonder the plant has won its name by its fruit rather than its flowers! Anyone might pass by the dull white bloom, but few could fail to notice the bunch of scarlet berries. And although they are insipid to our taste, many wild creatures find them wholesome food.

The bunchberry grows plentifully wherever found. In our northern woods it carpets the ground in great patches. Many of these plants are sterile, however, bearing only four leaves. The fertile plants have always six leaves in the centre, out of which rises the stalk with its bunch of scarlet fruit.

We found the bird life even more fascinating than the flowers. There is an elusiveness about birds that adds greatly to their charm. We can study and admire the flowers at our leisure; often we catch but a fleeting glimpse of a bird. Then comes the tantalizing question, "What was it?"

There is no month to be compared with May for richness of bird life. Here in the northern forest it is at its fullest, for this is the summer home of many of our birds. Every hour we saw about us many kinds in full spring plumage. And from dawn till dusk the woods rang with bird music.

As we paddled across the lake we saw the loon, so typical of the northern waters—and heard his weird laugh. He is a strange bird. There is an air about him which recalls prehistoric times. Naturalists tell us that all life began in the sea. If so, the loon has not progressed very far. Though almost helpless on land he is thoroughly at home in the water, swimming with ease either on or beneath the surface and diving in preference to flying.

As we neared the shore we saw the active little spotted sandpiper running along the beach or teetering daintily on the smooth wet rock, whistling his "Ter-wee, ter-wee." Or we surprised the great blue heron which flapped off with a hoarse croak, dragging his long legs awkwardly behind him. Again a mother merganser might be cruising near the shore with her family of ten or twelve ducklings. At our approach away they would all go pattering across the surface.

The toil of the portage was lightened by many an interesting incident. It would be a weary tramp indeed with a cumbersome canoe and a bulky pack if the woodland trail were not quick with life. And here we learned the value of knowing birds by their notes and songs.

High overhead there was a rose-breasted grosbeak singing. His mellow warble is unmistakable. A sharp two-noted whistle told us that the olive-sided flycatcher was astir. The rich song of the scarlet tanager came from the tree-tops. From the open woods we heard the languid call of the wood pewee. A pair of friendly chickadees twittered as they flitted from twig to twig. From the cool depths of the forest came the sweet, flowing song of the winter wren, sounding like a little rill trickling among the rocks and ferns. And from far and near we heard the plaintive tremulous whistle of the white-throat, the singer so typical of the north. All this came to our ears as we trudged along, yet we did not see a single bird. Through the woods thus ringing with music the trail wound, until the hoarse laugh of the loon announced the next lake and the mellow twitter of the swamp sparrow its reedy shore.

But these were birds of the noon-tide, sprightly singers of the sunny hours. As evening approached another class of songster was heard—the thrushes with their tender notes and more solemn songs. Often after a day of portageing and paddling, when camp was set up for the night and the evening meal finished, as one would go for a stroll in the city, we would go for a paddle. As we drifted along the rocky shore-line, with not a breath of wind stirring and a deep stillness over all, the western sky aglow and its colours gloriously reflected in the glassy lake, we listened to the songs of the thrushes from the depths of the forest. The clear bell-like notes of the wood thrush, the warbled song of the olive-backed thrush, the weird strains of the veery, and the calm, leisurely refrain of tender music from the hermit thrush—all these were combined into a harmonious chorus so in keeping with this peaceful setting. And as night closed in we heard the eerie hooting of the barred owl or the great horned owl, with the oft-repeated chant of the whippoorwill.

Although on our trip we had experiences much like those of Champlain, yet how very different the motive! Picture the energetic French voyageur, full of imagination and vision, urged on by his own restless spirit to seek out what might be beyond, leading, perhaps driving, his men both white and red onwards toward some unknown goal, braving heat and cold, fatigue and foes, storm and starvation—in fact every privation except thirst, for here, in this water-blessed country of Canada, I doubt if any traveller ever suffered from thirst. With all these problems constantly with him, we can well imagine that Champlain's canoe trips were no pleasure jaunts.

Compare for a moment his trips with ours of to-day. How ridiculously easy for us! We pack up our supply of well-assorted food and a carefully chosen outfit, and paddle and portage a light canoe through what we are pleased to call "wild country" by means of a modern map. We have little chance of getting seriously lost, and none of meeting hostile Indians, knowing all the while where we are going and when we will return.

Three hundred years with all its changes separate Champlain's romantic and strenuous experiences from our own prosaic modern trips, and yet nature herself has changed but little. We may not journey through the virgin forest with its pristine abundance of wild life. Man has altered all that. Yet it is impressive to reflect that the great explorer, as he paddled along over a northern lake with his red companions, probably looked out from his canoe at the loons and listened just as we did to their wild laughter. And as he trudged over the portage he heard the same ringing whistle of the olive-sided flycatcher. And, in his leisure moments, if he ever had any after the toils of the day, he listened with the same solemn pleasure to the restful music of the thrushes. And perhaps he was awakened by the hooting of the owl and the chanting of the whippoorwill, just as we were. And we have reason to believe that not one note of any of these voices of the wild which we hear today has changed from those which Champlain heard in those far-gone years of the sixteen hundreds.

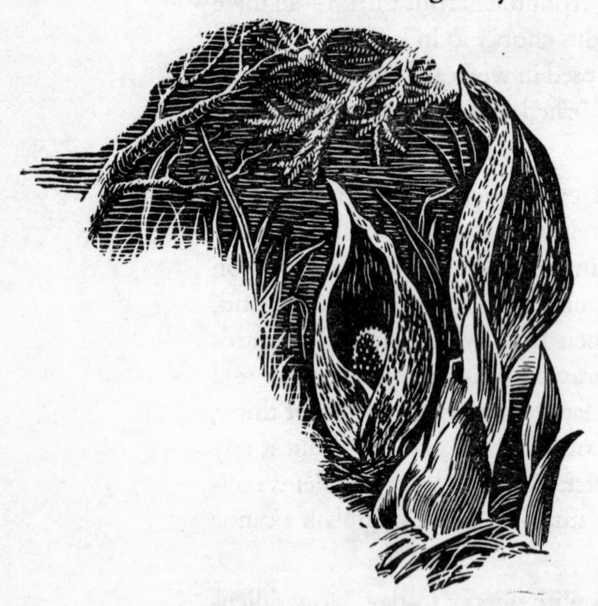

Mention of the wild flowers we saw on our trip brings to mind summer scenery, gaudy colours and sweet scents. But let me tell you of a flower which blooms so early in the spring that the snow may still be on the ground, which has no gaudy colours and certainly no sweet scent, and with a name as strange as its habits—the skunk cabbage.

This queer plant is growing long before you think of looking for wild flowers. About the middle of March this hardy pioneer has forced its way through the mud and before the end of the month is "blooming." It may not have much encouragement from the weather, a late fall of snow may bury it completely, yet the sturdy plant persists as though it were sure of itself and knew it could outlast the snow. It may find itself growing beside a patch of soiled spring ice, yet undaunted it sticks to its task of growing and unfolding in the March sunshine which is all the while melting the ice away.

And what a strange place it has chosen to grow and bloom! In a wet, muddy valley where all is tangled brush and where the trickling streamlets of the melting snows of the nearby hillsides are draining in. Surely there is nothing to tempt a plant to grow here! But then there is nothing to tempt a plant to grow anywhere at this time of year. The fields are still flooded with the water of the dirty dwindling snow. The woods are still deep in snow, for the sun's rays come but feebly through the network of naked branches overhead. But in this muddy little nook, sheltered from the March wind and into which the sun can pour his warmth, is the cosiest spot of all outdoors. So here nature brings forth her first sign of quickening life, her promise of better days—the homely skunk cabbage.

And he certainly is a homely fellow. At first glance you might easily pass him by. All that there is to be seen is a dull brownish-purple curled spike sticking through the wet mud. One side of this spike is open. Away inside is a stout round knob beset with yellow prickles. This knob is the flower proper. It always looks to me like the giant's club we read of in those weird tales of "Jack the giant-killer." The flower is now blooming and will soon go to seed. The thick curled spike around it is only the hood for protection. On the whole it does not require much imagination to see where the name "cabbage" comes in.

Now for the skunk part of the name. It is not because the plant has a skunk for a neighbour, nor that the prowling skunk feeds upon the plant. Just step over and break off a piece of that curly hood. At once a rank, powerful odour arises, a ghastly un-plant-like smell which resembles nothing so much as a nearby skunk in all his fragrant glory. There are but a few flowers in the woods which actually smell bad and the skunk cabbage is one of them. Yet rank as it is, curiosity impells me to smell it again each spring. There is something inexplicably attractive about its fetid aroma. And later in the season this same aroma reminds us vividly of the season we all love so well—genial spring with its quickening life.

But where is the rest of the plant? Has it nothing but a flower? So far, yes. The skunk cabbage, early as it is in the season, sets about without delay at the business of blooming. Yet if you look closely beside the hooded flower, you will find one or two sharp green points barely showing through the mud. These are the tightly folded leaves. As the flower blooms and fades these grow up higher and higher until they are far above the ground. Then, opening wider and wider, they become the largest leaves found in the woods, quite unlike what one would expect from so humble a flower. But different though they be, the leaves never lose the family taint. Crush one and you will at once smell the same fetid odour as in the flower. Again later in the season you have an opportunity of reminding yourself, as with the flower of early spring days.

Some day in May or June you may pass a little valley and find it handsomely decked out with a luxuriant growth of large bright green leaves, and wonder where the flowers are and when they will bloom. You are too late now to learn the secret of the skunk cabbage. You should have come in the first warm days of spring to discover the little curled hood with its hidden flower within.

There are some birds which, though they must feel the irresistible stir of spring, do not burst forth into song. I believe they would if they could, but nature has denied them musical voices, so in response to this all-powerful urge, they perform some of the strangest actions accompanied by the weirdest wing-music known in the bird world.

One of these is the woodcock, a long-legged, long-billed bird of a rich brown colour delicately mottled with buffs and greys. He prowls about the damp thickets probing the soft earth for his meal of earthworms. Another is a similar bird, Wilson's snipe or the jacksnipe; in fact he is related to the woodcock, as one could guess by his long legs and long bill. But we find him haunting the open grassy swamp, where his striped plumage serves to conceal him amid the herbage.

As you know from our week-end outdoors, the woodcock expresses his emotion in spring by performing what is known as his "sky-dance." Years before I had made the acquaintance of this sombre haunter of the thickets, but at first he was but a brown form which sped away before me on whistling wings as I startled him in his damp domain. In time, when I became better acquainted, I learned that this whistling was but a sample of his famous wing-music.

Strangely enough, it happened that in the very same month, but in quite another part of the country, I heard Wilson's snipe also performing *his* sky-dance. He is not so sedate a bird as the woodcock nor is his so finished a dance. Yet it is interesting to note that these two night-prowlers of the swales and thickets have a very similar way of expressing their feelings in spring.

I did not have friends to point out to me the actions of the snipe. In fact I was thoroughly puzzled by his music, when I first heard it. I was at the time near a low second-growth swamp in the evening and heard coming from some place a strange rapid bleating sound on the rising scale. The sound was repeated in the same way and same tone but never from the same place. Daylight had almost faded so that there was but the remotest chance of my being able to locate the source of the sound even had I been right in the swamp. Was it an owl? Or a raccoon? Or some night creature unknown to me? Such a sound might prove to be anything and so presented an alluring problem. I will come to-morrow in daylight, I thought, and unravel this mystery of the voice in the darkness.

Accordingly the following day I came to the spot and waded into the swampy thicket. It was a beautiful day. Nature, after her sleep of winter, was coming into her own. The willow buds were bursting, the yellow alder catkins were hanging full of rich pollen. The song sparrow and the chickadee were seen and heard on every side. As I was bending over some pond life which had attracted my notice, I heard the same unmistakable rapid bleeting call that had puzzled me on the previous evening. How fortunate that it should sound again in broad daylight! This meant some chance of solving the mystery. But where was the maker of this strange sound? As before it was repeated many times but never twice from the same spot. Now close at hand, then farther away, then still farther but from a different quarter, and now close at hand again. One might easily be deceived into believing that "the woods were full of them." But for the experienced searcher of strange sounds which seem to come from all directions there is but one place to look—upwards.

I did so. High above me in the clear sky was a bird in flight. Around and around he flew in wide reckless dashing circles that swung him over the expanse of the swamp below. I trained my field-glasses on him eagerly. The streaked plumage and the very long bill told me his name at once—Wilson's snipe. But the note, that rapid bleating, was it vocal or mechanical? I studied his actions more closely and noticed that as he drooped in flight he exerted more wing power to recover his speed. A few rapid wing-strokes increased his momentum and brought him upward again to the higher level, and with each of these accelerations came the mysterious sound that had so puzzled me the evening before. Thus I learned the sky-dance of the Wilson's snipe.

Spotted fawn
Sapsucker
Cicada

One of the greatest thrills you can have in the woods is to come upon a baby deer. The little creature is so un-deerlike that you might be pardoned for wondering what animal you have found. It is about the size of a small dog, with long slim legs, dainty little hoofs and mild dreamy eyes. The most remarkable thing about a baby deer is its spotted coat. The rich brown background of its fur is sharply marked with large white spots. This is quite unlike the coat of its parents; in fact different from any other animal in the woods.

We cannot help wondering why Nature ever should have given such a helpless creature such a startling coat. But is it startling? No colour scheme could afford more protection as long as the little deer lies still and quiet. The bright May sunshine gleams through the leafy trees, lighting up the forest floor with a multitude of sharply-checkered bright spots amid the shadows. The little deer may lie anywhere upon the ground in plain view and yet be quite invisible, due to nature's wise pattern of colour. And it seems to know that it is invisible, for it will lie perfectly still in

the presence of danger, even permitting itself to be handled without fright.

One of the experiences that remains as a gem in my memory occurred one bright spring day when I found a baby deer in the woods. A certain club of naturalists, to which I belong, went for a day's visit to a swamp, where we knew the great blue herons were nesting in a colony. After a long search we found the heronry could be reached only by three miles' walking and wading in the swampy country. We found scores of herons' nests, looking like great bundles of sticks in the tree-tops high overhead. We were much interested in the huge awkward birds which were standing by the nests or flapping through the air above the trees. It did seem strange that a big ungainly bird such as a heron should choose such a precarious site for a home, when he himself is so much a bird of the ground.

As we were returning homeward, wet to the knees, tired, hungry but very happy, those who were in front heard a shout from the rear of the line. We came back and were delighted to find a baby deer resting on one of the earthy islands of the swamp. It was so nearly invisible, as it lay in its spotted coat in the checkered lights and shadows of the forest, that most of us had walked right past it at almost an arm's length.

The beautiful little creature paid no attention to us as we gathered around it, not even resisting when we stroked its smooth fur, but how came this helpless thing to be alone unguarded in the midst of a huge wild swamp? I have no doubt that its mother was not far off, watching us in alarm. But her baby suffered no harm at our hands. We all paused, admired its beauty, stroked its dainty lithe form and left it nestled in its woodland cradle none the worse for our finding it.

That was a glorious day. Hour after hour we were surrounded by nature. There was bird life in all its beauty of song and plumage on every side. We saw many four-foots, too—squirrels, rabbits, weasels, muskrats and porcupines. Interesting swamp and woodland plants appeared wherever we went, but none of these gave us the same thrill as finding that tiny fawn, lying so helpless and yet so kindly shielded from harm and from enemy eyes by its strangely marked coat. And now that the ramble is passed and become but a memory, as I write these lines I wonder how many other helpless little fawns we passed that day and did not see at all.

But not all nature's strangely clothed creatures are hidden in the deep woods. Just outside my window there is a fine sugar-maple tree. It is many years old, for the bark of the trunk is old and furrowed, but the limbs and trunk higher up opposite the window are smooth and silvery grey. One spring morning I noticed that this smooth bark had been drilled by some sharp instrument; there were rows of neat holes in a regular pattern and the grey bark was dark with running sap. Who could have done this? Surely no boy would climb high up a tree for sap, and the black squirrels nibble off buds and twigs but do not gnaw bark. Someone had discovered the secret of the maple and was tapping the tree for its sap.

It was not long before I discovered who it was, for shortly after I happened to be looking out the window, when suddenly there appeared before my very eyes the queerest-looking creature you ever saw. He seemed to come from nowhere, just whirled himself into existence, like an acrobatic clown from some nearby trapeze, and alighted safely on the tree-trunk. He wore a strange coat of mottled black and white. His vest was pale yellow showing a huge bib as though he had come ready to dine. His throat was vivid scarlet, so was the little skull-cap he wore. One bar of white ran all the length of his wing. In books he is called the "Sapsucker," but I would not have been surprised if you had guessed anything else when such a garish-looking object flopped into view and settled in such an un-birdlike posture on an upright perch. You would have been inclined to laugh as we all do at the clown at the circus.

In fact he is the clown of the woodpecker family. His costume is most eccentric and quite unlike the dress of any of his relatives. His habits are different too, for he is the only toper of the family. Somehow he has learned the secret of my maple tree, and I don't doubt of several other trees in the neighbourhood. And now he spends his time going from one to another drinking deeply. His motto it seems is: "Be gay while the sun shines and the sap flows." But he himself is never gay. In spite of his gaudy costume and deep drinking he is always sober—very sober. Sapsucking is a very serious affair with him. It is his bread and butter for the most part. But of course he cannot live by sap alone. As we watch him we learn his little game. Sometimes in the warm sunshine certain insects, such as bees, wasps and flies, come uninvited to the feast, and of course our friend the sapsucker is not averse to a change of diet between sips of liquid.

For some time he remained at my tree solemnly drinking. Without a note, a flit of his tail or a toss of his head, he thrust his bill deep into the holes he had drilled, sipping the sap as quickly as it flowed for him. Then as suddenly as he had appeared he vanished, bound, I suppose, for the next tree.

The next day he was back at my maple. But something had happened overnight. The elves of frost had been abroad, and today no sap was running. All had frozen into icy crystals. It was as though nature had put our bibulous friend on the "Indian list." But was he to be denied? Not he. He seemed to say, "Very well, if I can't have sap to drink, I'll take water-ice, maple flavour, if you please." And his sharp little bill pecked away at the ice.

And now a strange little scene took place. Several English sparrows sat on the nearby branches and showed great interest in the sapsucker. I could hardly wonder at their interest in so comic a figure, garbed as he was so differently from themselves. But I soon learned that it was his actions, rather than his garb, that interested the sparrows. For when he, with his usual abruptness, left the tree they flew down, and clinging sideways to the bark in the most un-woodpecker-like pose, deliberately ate the sap-ice.

I cannot recall having seen any of our native birds eating the frozen sap provided by the sapsucker. This was clearly a case of observation and of following example. And I could not help reflecting that this little incident revealed how we often find that a foreigner coming to a new country—the English sparrow is not a native species with us—will see and, in a resourceful way, avail himself of an opportunity where others fail. That the English sparrow has done well in America cannot be denied.

In many families there is one member just a little different from the others. He may be a genius or a black sheep. John Burroughs was the only naturalist-author among a family of "plain folks." The woodpeckers are a family of patient, plodding, unimaginative birds, climbing trees, pecking into the bark for their food of insects, nesting in holes, and laying pure white eggs; and none of them are truly musical. The sapsucker is a woodpecker having all these characteristics in common with his brethren. But by what strange quirk in his history has he acquired this unique trait of deliberately tapping trees in spring to secure drink? True, this habit of his has marred many a tree trunk, but surely we can forgive him, for do not we ourselves tap the maples every spring for their sap to make our maple syrup and sugar?

But nature abounds in wonderful oddities. This reminds me of the time a friend told me of a very strange bug he had caught which thoroughly puzzled him. He was not very clear in detail when he described it to me except to say that it was very ugly.

Now, my friend is not a naturalist. So I hardly expected him to be very accurate in his description, and, as with most people all creeping things are spoken of as "bugs," I thought I had better reserve judgement as to what the creature might be until I saw it —although I had a good idea as to its identity. In a day or so, as promised, I received a small box, which I found contained a full-grown cicada and its empty shell.

I have a specimen before me now, and, as I tell you what is it like, you can picture it for yourself. It is about one and a quarter inches long, broad and stout, with a head as wide as its tubby body. On either side of this bullet-shaped head there is a big bulging eye. Instead of a mouth I see it has a sharp beak. It has six legs armed with claws and four wings which stretch far beyond its short body. Its colour is dull green and black worked into a queer pattern on the back. Altogether I cannot help thinking that my friend was correct in saying it is ugly.

As I look at the creature I am reminded of a little jingle you may have heard, and which I can well imagine the cicada saying:

For beauty I'm not a great star,
There are others more handsome by far.
My face, I don't mind it
Because I'm behind it—
It's you folks in front that I jar.

Perhaps you are thinking that you have never seen such an oddity. Probably not. The cicada is seldom seen. But I venture to say that almost everyone since he ever heard anything outdoors has listened to the song of this grotesque musician. His is one of the commonest notes in nature during the summer months, in fact the cicada is chief among the midsummer insect musicians. His song consists of a loud high-pitched ringing buzz continued sometimes fully half a minute uninterrupted, then dying away in a hoarse rattle. So familiar is this sound, and so associated with summer days, that the singer is known throughout the land as the "hot weather bug."

Like other insects of its order, the cicada has six legs, four wings, and its mouth parts fitted for piercing and sucking, not biting and chewing. As for its name, I find two sources, one Italian: "Cicada —an insect having a stout body and long wings." The other is Latin: "Cicada—a grasshopper, but now applied to certain large, noisy bugs, including the seventeen-year locust."

The cicada is a remarkable insect in a number of ways. First let's consider his song. There is something wonderful in the way in which this humble insect, a little over an inch long, can make its voice heard more than half a mile away. We all know the sound. We have heard it since we were old enough to rejoice in the coming of the summer holidays. But how many of us know how this music is produced? Perhaps I spoke a little too hastily in speaking of the insect's music as its "voice." The cicada has no voice, nor does it sing.

It was years before I had a chance to see for myself how the sound is made. The one summer day I was fortunate enough to catch a full-grown cicada in all his noisy glory. Generally when caught he sulks and won't perform, but this one buzzed continuously and I believe indignantly. I took him indoors at once, so he could not escape. Then, with a hand lens, I looked him over carefully in spite of his indignant buzzing. At first I was puzzled. The source of the music was not as obvious as I expected. Then I discovered on his body, under his gauzy wings, two little disks, one on each side. These seemed to have something to do with the sound. I examined them very closely and found them to be tightly stretched membranes like tiny drums. When the insect was buzzing they were seen to be vibrating very rapidly, but so minutely that I could detect the movement only with my lens.

Then, in order to satisfy myself that these membranes were beyond doubt the insect's musical instruments, I took a pin and punctured each. After that not a sound came from the insect no matter how I handled him. Without the drum-membranes the cicada was incapable of a single note.

To explain this I may use a crude simile. Imagine a large tin pan, the bottom of which gives a sharp metallic snap when pressed, and another when released. Should two such pans be pressed in and out very rapidly and made to sound alternately—that is, the beats of one filling in the spaces of the other—the result would be a continuous rattle as of a kettle-drum. And so rapidly can the cicada vibrate his drumheads that the resulting sound is the high, shrill buzz known to all.

The cicada is remarkable in another way. He has a unique life history. You will recall that I spoke of him as the "seventeen-year locust." It may seem surprising that this active insect, sporting about and singing his song with such vigour on hot summer days, is just enjoying the final stage of his existence. Years ago he began life as an egg which was laid on a shrub. The grub which emerged dropped to the ground and at once began to dig himself in. Down, down he burrowed into the soft earth, living upon the juices of roots. Season after season went by and still the little grub remained below, burrowing and growing. Perhaps some time when you were digging in your garden you may have brought to light a soft white grub and wondered what it was. It was an immature cicada.

After many seasons of feasting this grub underwent a change of form and became somewhat more like the mature insect as we know him. And now he felt the urge to live upon a higher plane.

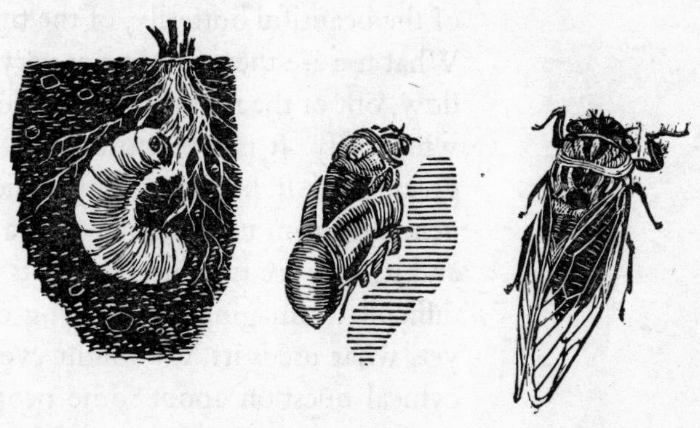

Nature prompted him to burrow upward towards the light of day. His long apprenticeship was ended; now he was to become a fully developed cicada, living in the open air and sunshine, able to fly about and make the summer air resound with his music.

So, this humble monk of the cloister came forth from his cell, crawled up the nearby stalk and paused to await nature's bidding. Then a strange thing happened. The skin of his back split, and out from his old self he crawled, and stood forth a full-grown cicada with eyes and wings and a pair of tiny drums, leaving behind the empty shell—the shape of the earthly thing he used to be.

But he was still woefully callow and limp. He must linger in the sun and air for a few minutes while Nature put on the finishing touches. In those few minutes his wings stiffened, his colour changed from pale brown to jet black and dark green. His musical instruments hardened and were ready to vibrate. He had become what nature intended him to be—a mature cicada.

Yet, in spite of all, his looks did not improve. And he is still as my friend described him—ugly. And as I look at the specimen in my hand, with its ungainly shape, its bullet-shaped head and great bulging eyes and crooked beak, he certainly is the hobgoblin of the insect world. How poorly he compares with any of our many butterflies with their gorgeous spread of wings, so wonderfully covered with microscopic scales of vivid hues! Or some of our brilliant beetles with their metallic colours like burnished gold, silver and bronze. And yet all these beauties have been through a similar stage to that of the cicada of lowly birth.

Perhaps at this point you are tempted to ask of the cicada, "What use is it?"—this ugly insect which took so long to develop. But could not the same question be asked of any of nature's creatures—of the beautiful butterfly, of the tiny ant or the mighty elephant? What use are they all? At this very moment, in through my window, out of the night, there has flown onto my copy here, a lace-winged fly. It is a beautiful little insect. Its body is a pale fresh green hue. It has four long delicate lace-like wings with fine veining. From its head, it waves a pair of long graceful antennae and its eyes are two brilliant spots of burnished gold. It would be difficult to imagine a tiny being of more exquisite beauty. And yet, what use is it? We might even go so far as to ask the same cynical question about some people, even among our own acquaintances.

Well, nature is not a bit concerned as to our attitude regarding her creatures. Neither has she placed anything in this world for our admiration or entertainment. From the least unto the greatest, from the ugliest unto the most beautiful, each is planned to fit into its place and, in a wonderful way, to be part of her great scheme of things. And I, for one, would sadly miss the harsh strident song of the cicada, just as I would the soft dreamy note of the wood pewee, the liquid warbling of the red-eyed vireo, the drowsy hum of the bee and a score of other sounds in nature which make up the music of midsummer.

Unbidden guests
The dying lake

Ramble five

ONE lovely spring day as I was passing a little patch of woods I heard a yellow warbler singing. Do you know the bird? He is the little warbler with the bright golden-yellow plumage, his breast streaked with chocolate brown. His lively twitter is heard in May just when your garden is at its best. That sprightly song always recalls to me "lilac time." Almost all our warblers pass on to the far north to nest but the yellow warbler is one of the few which remain with us in Southern Ontario throughout the summer. You may find him nesting in your garden.

On hearing this familiar song in such a promising location and at this time of year, what was more natural than to step into this little woodland and search for the nest? I knew just what to look for—a neat compactly built bundle of plant fibres, lined with down. The woodland was composed mostly of small cedars and willows, whose ripening catkins were shedding their silky down into the air. Just the thing this bird would use to line the nest. So, with these encouraging signs I looked about, peering into this thicket and that, slapping mosquitoes all the while, and after a few minutes' search I found what I sought—the nest of the yellow warbler.

It was six feet from the ground almost hidden in a tangle of twigs where a cedar and willow mingled their foliage. And, that I might make no mistake as to whose home I had found, not far off the little warbler herself was chirping her protest at my intrusion.

Now, to find a nest is simple enough. In fact many birds almost tell you their home is nearby in their alarm. But a nest found is a task only half done. You should learn much more about it. So, I drew myself gently up and peered into the little home. Eggs, sure enough. Little speckled eggs; but what a lot of them—six. This is an unusual number for the yellow warbler. But wait, one of the eggs is larger than the others and differently speckled. There now. If you know our birds you will have guessed the secret. The odd egg is not a yellow warbler's at all but a cowbird's.

And what is a cowbird? And how did a cowbird's egg get into the nest of a yellow warbler? Well, now let me tell you a strange piece of nature lore, one of the little dramas of the bird world. A drama which, though often a tragedy, sometimes turns out to be a comedy.

Many of our song birds, such as sparrows, warblers, vireos, blackbirds and thrushes, feed upon insects; so we speak of them as "beneficial" birds. But among them there is one which we call a villain. This is the cowbird. Of course he is not really a villain, he is just one of nature's birds as are all the others. But we don't like him. Have you ever noticed that in plays the villain is generally of a dark complexion and dressed in dark clothes? The cowbird's plumage is greenish black and he has a dark brown head. We don't like his plumage or his gurgling song.

Still, we might forgive him his gloomy garb and sullen song, but for the habits of his mate. In spring, when all other birds are busy with their nesting duties, we find the female cowbird sneaking about the bushes looking for the nest of some smaller species into which she can slip one of her eggs. So secretive is she in doing this that few people have seen her in the act.

Once the egg is thus deposited she bids good-bye to the whole affair. Then the trouble begins. The strange egg is hatched and the young cowbird is fed and cared for by its foster parents, who never seem to realize that they are being imposed upon; the intruder grows and grows until he crowds the rightful occupants out of the nest. In fact sometimes he actually heaves them out by force.

Even after the young cowbird is able to fly it is a common sight to see a pair of smaller birds feeding a big husky fledgling as tenderly as though he were their own. And is he grateful? Not he. As soon as his wings can bear him well, off he goes and joins the cowbird flocks which we see feeding in the stubble fields in September. Think of all the disturbed, perhaps broken, homes these huge flocks represent. This is the tragedy.

Now, for the comedy. The yellow warbler is a bright little bird. Her eye and her brains are as bright as her plumage. One day she comes back to her nest to find that a strange egg has been slipped in during her absence. What does she do? Some birds would not notice anything amiss. Others would and as a result desert the nest and begin housekeeping all over again elsewhere. But the sly little yellow warbler begins at once to build another nest over the first, leaving the cowbird's egg down below. Should she find herself imposed upon the second time she will add a third storey. I have found two-storey nests and seen photographs of three, and even four and five-storey nests. And what stories those storeys could tell! So the cunning little warbler sets at nought the efforts of the obnoxious cowbird and turns what might have been a tragedy into a comedy.

Now, I can imagine I hear some English friend say, "Why the cowbird has the same objectionable habit as our English cuckoo!" True; and strange, is it not, that two birds of widely different

families, living in continents separated by three thousand miles of ocean, have learned the same sly habit of evading home duties and family responsibilities? How does it happen thus? In what strange way did they ever learn the same habit? Some day a naturalist may arise who will enlighten us on this and many other mysteries and secrets in the life histories of our birds which puzzle us.

The English cuckoo is a fairly large bird with a long tail. He is more often heard than seen. And, as is the case with such birds, he has become surrounded with a certain air of mystery. As the poet says:

O Cuckoo! shall I call thee bird,
Or but a wandering voice?

I have rarely seen an English cuckoo myself, but when in England I frequently heard the birds calling from the woods and hedgerows of those lovely English counties of Kent, Surrey, Sussex and Hampshire. The note is very easily imitated, as has been ingeniously done in the mechanism of the cuckoo clock. As the schoolboy said, "The cuckoo is the bird that imitates the cuckoo clock."

This brings to mind the story of the man who came home very late one night. In fact it was three o'clock in the morning. Perhaps he was a naturalist. Naturalists stay out very late sometimes when there is anything of interest to see or hear. Well, just as he stepped in the door the clock "cuckooed" three times, and he, with great presence of mind, "cuckooed" nine times more to make the hour sound more respectable to his wife, who he knew would be listening for him. I might say that we have no cuckoo clocks in our home, though we have two naturalists.

In the east we have two species of cuckoo—the yellow-billed and the black-billed. Both are slim birds with long tails, white breasts, and brown backs. Like the English bird, they have surrounded themselves with an air of mystery. We seldom have a good look at a cuckoo. We may hear him call but as we approach he slips out of the thicket and away. Both are shy secretive birds. Yet they have nothing to be ashamed of for their habits are very beneficial. One of their favorite foods is the tent caterpillar which spins that disfiguring nest of cobweb so often seen on the shrubbery of the roadside. Very few birds will eat hairy caterpillars. You see they are afraid of being "tickled to death." But the cuckoos devour these pests wholesale so we would be better off if we had more cuckoos.

There is a marked similarity between the old-world and the new-world cuckoo as I mentioned. In appearance, in voice and in general habits we can readily see the relationship. But strange to say our cuckoos, unlike their English cousins, have learned to build their own nests and care for their own young. You see a long time ago they were sent out to this new country to reform, as were many people. And they have at least learned one good lesson. Yet the family taint persists, for our cuckoos build very flimsy nests not to be compared with the dainty substantial home of the yellow warbler for example.

But we mustn't be too hard on our cuckoo. He is still in his apprenticeship. Strange to tell, it is said that cuckoos have a regrettable fall from grace. Occasionally one of them will slip an egg into a neighbour's nest. And by the same token the eggs she herself hatches out may not all be her own. A nice neighbourly custom I call it, this borrowing and lending additions to families, isn't it? No one should object to that surely. Here again the remarkable fact is revealed, that, in spite of the wide stretch of ocean between two species, the family weakness is apparent—or should I say "a parent"?

In any case it is interesting to compare this irresponsible method of nesting as we find it in two birds a half a world apart with the careful way in which the robin, the song sparrow, the yellow warbler and most of our birds select a site, gather material and skilfully construct their nests and tenderly care for their young. We feel that nature must be remiss in some way when we compare such differences in habits.

Perhaps we feel too that we should take a hand in the matter and put things right. But we should be very cautious in our interfering in any of nature's affairs. I recall that when I was a boy a well-meaning, though as I now know a misinformed, friend advocated destroying cowbirds' eggs at every opportunity, saying he always took them from other nests whenever he found them. Yet I remember on one occasion I found an Indigo bunting's nest and again a goldfinch's, both with cowbirds' eggs in them. Acting on my friend's counsel I took the strange eggs out and in both cases the birds deserted their nests. I thought I knew better than nature, but I didn't.

Some day, perhaps, we shall learn that nature knows best. Cowbirds have been living with the rest of our native birds now for countless generations, and for aught we know they may be very beneficial birds, which we should sadly miss if exterminated. And it certainly would be a tragedy for us to realise this when it is too late.

Have you ever come across a dying lake? This is a strange thing to say, surely. We usually think of a lake as a cool, refreshing spot and blessed with abundant life—in fact, anything but dying. What is a dying lake then?

Imagine a sheet of sparkling fresh water nestled in hilly country. Each spring the freshets pour into the lake and all through the summer the trickling streams find their way in, slowly filling it up with their sediment. Year after year this filling process goes on until the lake becomes quite shallow.

In this shallow water many kinds of aquatic plants take root and thrive. There are the well-known cattails, with their brown heads and narrow leaves; tall, waving sedges and grasses; the purple pickerel-weed with its pointed, curly leaves; the pink water persicaria; the white marsh calla; the much-sought-after water lilies, both white and yellow, with their broad, floating leaves; and the least of all flowering plants, the duckweed, covering the surface as a green scum. Even below the surface there are the eel grass and the chara, strange plants that grow and bloom under water.

Season after season these all grow, flourish and, in dying, sink to the bottom making fresh soil. Thus is the lake gradually filled up with an accumulation of its own dead vegetation, until at last the whole area becomes a broad expanse of damp vegetable-mud. The lake has vanished. In its place there is now a level meadow of grass and sedge.

This may take years and years, even centuries, to come about. For like many another process in nature this is very slow.

There are many dying lakes throughout the country. We often see them as we drive along. Some appear as clear pools covered with water plants, others as reedy marshes where little water is to be seen; or the process of filling up may have gone so far that the whole spot is a swamp of willow or alder bushes. But, at whatever stage of dying, such lakes are, unlike most things that are dying, always interesting and often beautiful.

Not long ago I enjoyed a visit to a dying lake. It was a pretty little spot several hundred yards in extent, nestling in a low area of a cultivated part of open country. All around the shore, if one could call it a shore, grew a dense tangle of willows. Then farther out there were acres of tall green grass. And in the very centre of the place lay a sheet of water dotted with white and yellow pond lilies.

I spent most of my time among the rushes, for the central part of open water, though shallow, was too deep for my hip-boots. For a couple of hours I prowled about in this green forest of waving vegetation, which was about as high as my head, finding many varieties of wild life, at almost every turn. Birds, large and small, nimble and ungainly, frogs, snakes and turtles and even some four-foots had made their homes amid this grassy jungle. Interesting folk, all of them. But though they were all living their own lives here together and had little to do with each other, I soon found that they had this in common—they one and all resented my presence. I was not welcome anywhere I went, and many did not hesitate to tell me so in their own way. They seemed to consider me a trespasser. Well, so I was. I had really no right to be in their domain, much less to be poking into their affairs and prying into their home life.

I had not gone very far into the reeds before I heard a hoarse note from nearby, "Kuh-kuh-kuh." There was nothing to be seen for all about me was a tangle of green. But I knew this sound to be the alarm note of a least bittern. I went in the direction of the note and soon found amid the reeds a very much perturbed bittern. In spring this could only mean one thing; the bird's nest must be near by. Yes, there it was, a mere flat platform of dead reeds a foot or so above the wet earth.

The nest was empty but clinging to the reeds above it, I found three of the most grotesque little creatures you could imagine. They were young bitterns and this was their first journey away from home, a couple of feet. They were covered with white down, their wing and tail feathers partly grown. It was amusing to see them clinging to the reeds with their long toes, holding their bills straight up or striking weak helpless blows at my hand when I came too near. I had my camera with me and took several pictures of this absurd little group.

Now as I was moving around to get these pictures in the best light, I happened to look down at my feet where to my surprise I found a brown animal. At first I thought it to be a muskrat, but one look at that hairy, not scaly, tail and I knew it to be a young woodchuck. He was as wet as a "drowned rat." I cannot imagine how a baby woodchuck, who should be on the dry upland pasture, came to be out here. He was clearly out of his element. Yet lost and wet as he was, there was plenty of fight in him. He braced himself and prepared to die game. When I gave him a poke he ground his teeth and bit savagely at my boot. But, though he doesn't know it, I have a couple of snaps of him in his sad plight. The next thing of interest that I came upon was a large water snake basking in the sun. I suppose I should tell you that he was "ten feet long if he was an inch." That is the way in which snakes are generally described. But this fellow was all coiled up, so it was hard to say. He, too, objected to my presence. He struck a couple of vicious harmless blows at my boot, then glided off to be lost among the grasses. As he went I noticed carefully and I am sure he was at least two feet long.

I was now getting onto wetter ground and found several nests of the marsh wren. These are interesting little structures, woven out of the long blades of marsh grass, attached to the upright stems. Some were completed and lined with the down of the cattail heads, others were a mere framework of a nest. Nearby I saw the little architect himself, a nervous bundle of feathers that chattered and scolded at me all the while.

Judging from the number of nests about one would conclude that there was a whole colony of marsh wrens living here. But the truth is that this energetic little bird actually builds nests just for the fun of it or for the pure joy of keeping busy. At least so it seems, for there are always far more nests than occupants.

And here, too, I found his neighbour, the red-winged blackbird. Two or three of these were flying overhead voicing their objections to my intrusion in clicks and whistles. Of course I knew the reason. More nests. One near at hand had five blue eggs curiously sprawled with black in it.

My rambling now brought me to a clear view of the open water of the marsh. There I saw a number of birds swimming about rather like ducks. But the odd nodding movement of their heads as they moved about told me they were coots. Some were smaller than others, and as I watched them I heard a soft cooing note. Before long I had guessed the secret. It was the father and mother coot out for a cruise with the family. The coot does not take her babies out for a walk as we do ours, but for a swim. There is no walking about a coot's home, in fact the baby coots are born on a raft.

As I watched them I was surprised by a scuffle in the water near at hand, and looked around to see a little pied-billed grebe swimming for the open water. On reaching it he mysteriously disappeared before my eyes. Of course I knew the trick. He simply sank below the surface and came up again near the reeds. No doubt he was watching as long as I was in sight. Had I scared a coot he would have scampered off through the tangle like a frightened hen, or perhaps pattered over the surface of the water. But the grebe is quite helpless among the reeds. Water is his element and his home. And he knew where to seek safety when he heard noisy footsteps approaching.

Just at this point I found myself in the midst of a flock of very excited black terns. They flew overhead in circles and swooped down at me, coming within a few inches of my head, all the while screaming their shrill cries. Clearly I was near their nesting site, I looked about on every side and found at least one nest. It was on a muddy little island, out of reach, surrounded by deep water. There was no chance of my getting a close-up view of that nest. The tern is a beautiful bird with a black body, ashy-grey wings, a sharp bill and a forked tail. Its long wings and forked tail at once mark it as an expert flier. In fact terns are very much the same shape as swallows and just as skillful on the wing. As I watched these graceful terns circle and soar, swoop and dive, I thought, "Surely theirs is the acme of perfection in flying."

There was an old turtle sunning himself on a floating island. The touches of crimson on his shell told me he was the variety known as the painted turtle. The moment I came close he flopped off into the water and vanished. Four black ducks I had noticed here a few minutes ago decided that I was getting too close and rose off the surface and flew away quacking. Here too a glum old American bittern jumped up suddenly from somewhere in the reeds and flapped across the pond with a dismal croak. I never felt less welcome anywhere; nobody at all seemed to want me near.

And now I came to the most interesting experience of the whole trip. I just happened to turn my head about and caught sight of what appeared to be a bit of fur hanging on the reeds. It was a least bittern posing. This bittern is a slim lanky bird with long neck, long bill and long legs. He is of the same suspicious disposition as his larger cousin the American bittern. When he sees trouble coming his way, his bid for safety is not in flight, either by foot or wing, but by simply posing. He stretches himself the full limit and hopes to pass as part of the scenery. And to make the most of this attitude he points his bill to the zenith. And he very nearly succeeded in escaping observation, for I had to look closely to be quite sure of my bird. The comical part of it all was that he fooled himself, for, so sure was he that he was invisible, that I actually stepped up closer and took two good snaps of him in this absurd posture. Then I happened to turn aside for a moment and when I looked back again he was gone. He had seen his chance and had "beat it while the beating was good."

Two hours had elapsed now since I had seen my companions. It was time to return to camp. I had had a most interesting time although it was hardly the place one would choose to have a picnic. Yet think of all the queer folk I had met that I never would have found in any other spot. But with all the croaks and squeals and grunts and quacks of protest, being snapped at by a woodchuck, struck at by a water snake and given the cold shoulder by a mud turtle, I had, as I have mentioned, reason to believe that I was not welcome.

Some day I hope to return and again visit this dying lake. It will be a long time in dying and when I come I shall probably see many of the same inhabitants, and perhaps some new ones. But slowly and surely the rank growth of vegetation is filling up the lake. In another fifty or a hundred years the place will be a broad flat valley with a fine stand of timber growing upon it. I should like very much to ramble through those woods then. Everything will be changed and quite different, but I'm sure will be equally interesting.

Trillium
Indian pipe
Wintergreen
A warbler's song
Eclipse of the sun

ONE of the most glorious flowers in our woods in spring. is the white trillium. There are many more brightly coloured and many with sweeter perfume, but the trillium has a charm of its own. It may be the purity of its snowy whiteness, its modest bearing or its generous size; or perhaps the glorious effect produced by hundreds growing together. Whatever the reason, this splendid flower has won an undisputed place in our affections.

May is trillium month. The earliest days of spring with the thrill of finding the first wild flowers is past, and as yet it is not summer with flowers everywhere. The trillium, then, has a little season of its own when it may bloom and claim our attention.

Though belonging to the lily family, the trillium differs in some respects from other members of this well-known group. The flower is so called because its parts are all in threes. Three leaves, three sepals, three petals; to the botanist this speaks volumes. He knows that all lilies are made up on this three-fold plan. The trillium then must belong to the family. But—and here is the

puzzle—lilies have straight-veined leaves; those of the trillium are criss-crossed or net-veined. Why this exception? It would seem as though nature has deliberately put this little catch in her well-ordered scheme of things so we will not learn our botany too easily.

The large white trillium of the woods is not the only one of its kind. Standing six to eight inches high and opening fully five inches in extent to the May sunshine, she is undisputed queen. But there is another like her, a smaller trillium which seems to feel her place to be second for her head is drooping modestly below the leaves. Then there is the pretty little painted trillium with its white petals daintily streaked with purple. And curiously enough growing with the large white trillium we find the red variety, whose flower is dull purple-brown and has a disagreeable odour. This odour, of course, attracts flies which cannot resist alighting and scrambling about the flower. They get nothing for their pains for there is no food on the red trillium. But their scrambling stirs up the pollen and so fertilizes the flower to bring forth seed. In the same way, and with the same result, is the honey bee attracted by the scent of the white trillium. It does not really matter whether it is a bee or a fly that visits the flower, provided the pollen dust is stirred up.

About the twenty-fourth of May the trilliums are at their best in our woods. On the hillside in the checkered pattern of sunlight and shadow cast by the newly-leafed trees of the forest these glorious flowers grow in masses. There are few sights in the spring woods more pleasing than hundreds of trilliums thus blooming with their ample petals of snowy white. Day after day they brighten the forest in the sunshine, wholesome in their purity. But should you return a week or so later you will find every flower flushed with a dull pink. This is the hue of the fading trillium soon to go to seed.

In some localities the very beauty of this splendid flower has brought about its ruin. Thoughtless people, especially from cities, finding so lovely a bloom, gather it unsparingly, sometimes by the armful. Every year this destruction goes on, until now there are places where once the trilliums grew in thousands and today there is not a single plant. Had the trilliums thus gathered reached homes, there to be admired, it would not be so sad a story. But many were carelessly thrown aside on the roadside. So the children of today are denied the joy of seeing the splendid abundance of this glorious flower that once graced the hillsides. Surely this is a lesson for those of us who live nowadays to spare other flowers now abundant, that those come after us be not denied the wholesome pleasure of their beauty.

If you were asked what we associate most with wild flowers, I believe your answer would be colour. We admire the red of the poppy, the blue of the forget-me-not, and the yellow of the buttercup, and the colours of many other flowers when the flowers themselves are almost scentless. Colour seems to benature's gift to the plant world, and yet, strange to say, sometimes we find flowers denied this boon. True flowers they are, budding, blooming and ripening into seed; and yet so lacking in pigment that when first found in the woods they might be mistaken for some kind of fungus.

A very common example of these oddities is the Indian pipe. This plant grows in little groups in cool shady places under large forest trees. As its name suggests, it resembles a pipe with its curved stem and stout bowl. But I really think it looks more like a Dutchman's pipe than an Indian's. Of course the plant grows in the forest, where there are more likely to be Indians than Dutchmen. Most plants have more than one name, and the more unusual its appearance, the more names are bestowed upon it. And so Indian pipe, looking so weird and uncanny in its cold clammy whiteness, is also appropriately known as "corpse plant" and "ghost flower." Unlovely names are they not? Yet certainly very descriptive. But it is not lack of colour alone that makes Indian pipe such an odd plant. Its habit of growth is just as strange. Most plants obtain their nourishment from the soil and drink in the life-giving sunshine through their leaves. But Indian pipe belongs to a unique class called "saprophytes," which really means decay plants. These derive their food from decaying wood underground. In fact they live much as do toadstools. Little wonder then we find Indian pipe with the anaemic appearance so typical of the fungus family.

Of course, with all its colourless and grisly appearance, Indian pipe, like all plants, must have relatives and a family history. And many of these relatives are very beautiful, and some are universally known. To the botanist, they belong to the great family of heaths. The far-famed heather which tints the Scottish highlands; Labrador tea with its evergreen leaves covered with rusty wool below; Andromeda—for some fanciful reason named after the constellation—with its leaves gracefully curled at the edges; leather-leaf with its pretty little urn-like flowers, all plants of our northern swamps, are of the heath family. The fragrant wintergreen with its rich evergreen leaves and appetizing berries, the tasty cranberry on sale in grocery stores, the blueberry which makes such delicious pies and the delicate little snowberry trailing a thread-like vine along the ground bearing tiny white fruit—all these are heaths. And then there is a bog plant, named kalmia after a famous Swedish botanist who visited this country in the early years, whose showy pink flowers fairly set the sombre bog aglow with colour. And we must not forget to mention the beautiful rhododendron of the garden, another member of the heath family. So the lowly, colourless, clammy Indian pipe, outcast as it may seem, has many interesting and splendid relatives.

But why, we might ask, should such strange contrasts exist in one family? Why Beauty and the Beast so closely related? I am sure of Beauty, for each of the plants above mentioned, in design, in flower and in fruit has a beauty of its own. But I am not so ready to call Indian pipe the Beast. Rather let us speak of it as an interesting plant which by its very strange habits of living and its uncanny appearance tempts us to delve more deeply into nature's secrets.

Turning to one of the handsome members of the heath family, whenever you think of wintergreen, what comes to your mind? Chewing gum and candy? Why? Because many of these little luxuries are flavoured with this spicy substance.

Wintergreen is a unique little plant common in our North American woods. Although there is a whole family of plants bearing this name, only one has the distinct taste we know. The name refers to the fact that the leaves remain green all winter. Some time when you are out in the woods when the snow lies on the ground, dig down by some old stump and you may find a little shrub four or five inches high, with no flowers or fruit at this season, of course, but still bearing its green leaves. The leaves are not thin and flexible as most are, but thick and rigid and when bent almost crack apart. As the snow melts away in the spring, they appear bright green amid the brown debris of plant-life, as though already alive and growing. I suppose many people who found them thus believed that the plant had been growing beneath the snow and so the name "wintergreen" seemed natural. It is not to be confused with the term "evergreen" which is applied to many of our forest trees.

The flower of the plant is a delicate pink-and-white bell which hangs beneath the leaves. Inside this bell is what is termed the stigma, looking just like the tongue. But this little bell never rings. The plant gives forth its message in another way. The scarlet berry, which is pleasant to the taste, is called tea-berry. It seems that the early settlers made tea of the rich green leaves, speaking of the fragrant beverage as wintergreen tea. Thus the plant became known as "tea-berry wintergreen"—a roundabout method of arriving at a name, is it not?

But the humble little shrub has another and more distinguished title. Botanists have named it Gaultheria after a very celebrated court physician and naturalist at Quebec in the middle of the eighteenth century. Yet, though celebrated, the good doctor does not seem to have left us certain of the spelling of his name. In my botany I find this note, regarding the plant, "Name dedicated to Hugues Gaultier—also spelled Gaulthier, Gauthier and Gautier." And strange to say this name has been bestowed upon the plant by another distinguished naturalist, Peter Kalm, who travelled and studied in North America about that time. I fancy I can see these two old cronies of those by-gone days strolling off into Canadian forest—not too far, as they, of course, valued their precious scalps—and marvelling at the wealth of new-world botany around them.

I suppose that from earliest days the Indians have chewed wintergreen leaves and enjoyed their flavour. Perhaps Indian children gave the idea to the white settlers' children in those early days. However we may have learned the secret of the little plant, there are many people even to-day who, when strolling through the woods, still pluck a leaf of the wintergreen to nibble, and I am one of them. For to me its spicy flavour recalls to mind many long rambles in the woods enjoyed in former days.

We often hear the phrase "the eye of the naturalist." But no true naturalist depends on his eyes alone while afield. His ear is ever open to the sounds in the woods all about him. A veteran woodsman once told me that he looked for birds with his ears first and then saw them with his eyes. And the longer I go on nature rambles the more I find him to be right. One June day I had an experience which taught me the value of hearing as well as seeing.

It was a very hot day. I was out on a scrubby hillside. There were a few birds singing in the neighbourhood, and among these I caught the note of a warbler some distance away. At first the lively twitter sounded like the song of a yellow warbler. Yet the more I listened the more it became the song of the chestnut-sided warbler. These two little birds sing much alike.

But there was something not quite right about this chestnut-sided warbler's song. The emphatic note at the end of the song that rings out so clearly was lacking. This was certainly worth looking into. I had no difficulty finding so persistent a singer, even amid shrubbery. And soon I saw the reason for my doubt. The bird could not say his name out clearly for his bill was full of insects. How could he bring out that emphatic note so typical of his song when he must hold his bill tight shut?

A warbler gathering insects by the billful on a shrubby hillside in June—that could mean only one thing, a nest and nestlings near at hand. Otherwise he would have eaten those insects as fast as he caught them. I followed him from bush to bush until at last he led me to his secret. Into the depths of one of the bushes he flew and soon reappeared, without the insects.

Ah, in that bush lay the secret; and, as though to confirm this, the next minute the mother bird appeared on the scene, also with a billful of insects, dived into the bush and also came out without them.

I peered into the bush; and there, woven to the twigs of the purple-flowering raspberry vine, some three feet from the ground, was the little home. Three tiny half-fledged nestlings held up their wide baby bills to me to be fed. But it was not my work to feed them. That task I left to two busy little birds who knew far better than I what baby warblers should eat. I looked at them for a moment, wondering why there were not four, the usual number in a warbler family.

Weeks went by before I was again able to visit the little nest in the raspberry vine on the hillside. The merry twitter was heard no more. Three little warblers were flitting about feeding themselves by now. I took another look into the nest I had found. There at the bottom lay one solitary egg which had never hatched. Now I knew why I had found only three nestlings in the little family. Then I thought of how much I would have missed had I left unheeded the message my ears brought me on that hot June day on the hillside, and had not troubled to solve the riddle of the warbler's song that did not sound quite right.

But it was my eyes that brought me a little story with a big thought behind it.

Many years ago the eastern part of the North American continent witnessed an eclipse of the sun. Although it was total in a limited area only, thousands of persons provided themselves with smoked glasses through which to gaze on this rare phenomenon. At Toronto, my home, on that day the sky was cloudless so that we had an unobstructed view of the sight though only ninety-two per cent of the sun's disk was obscured. It seemed, too, that the eclipsing of the sun on this day was a kindly act of nature, for it was the hottest day of the whole summer. It was as though nature had relented her harshness and sought to make amends.

At twelve minutes past two a tiny bite could be seen in the round shape of the sun's disk. Gradually this crept across the surface until at twenty-four minutes after three only a thin bright crescent at the lower edge remained aglow where before stood the round fiery sun.

At this time the bright light of day had faded to a dull leaden glow, in which we could see the buildings and the foliage of the trees appearing in an unearthly gloom. It was as though the eerie twilight of a premature evening had settled over all, but with the full heat of noonday.

No wonder an eclipse of the sun filled the ancients and the mediaeval folk with fear and alarm! Even that day we could scarcely shake off the feeling of awe and wonder which gripped us as the moments wore on and the gloom became deeper—a feeling that something very unusual and awesome was happening. One could readily imagine this to be the preliminary to some mighty natural catastrophe.

For a brief half-hour or so the leaden twilight palled all, then, silently as it had come, the disk of the moon moved on and Old Sol became himself once more. And again all stood out in the golden light of the summer afternoon.

And now comes the strange irony of it all. On this day, August 31st, 1932, the whole country had watched the eclipse of the sun as described. Wonderfully foretold, awe-inspiring to behold, we saw before our very eyes the God-like intellect of man linked up with the majesty of nature. But of all those who, in the streets, in the parks and on the house-tops, gazed rapt at this eclipse of the sun, how many paused to admire the sunset of the following day? This was the most magnificent sunset seen for many a day. From the farthest north to the extreme south the whole western sky was a mass of glory. On the horizon, at a point where the sun had just set, hung a fringe of cloud vivid with flaming gold. Above this stood masses of clouds tinged in prodigal grandeur with scarlet, pink, purple, crimson, mauve and blue-grey. And through all this here and there were spaces showing the purest of transparent blues and greens of the clear sky itself as a background.

Yesterday all had gazed with intense interest on one tiny spot of sunlight; this evening half the sky was filled with glory, which if noticed at all was given by many but a casual glance. At the eclipse we all had marvelled; the sunset received but passing notice. True, an eclipse happens once in many years, the sunset daily. But suppose a glorious sunset were to occur only once in many years, then indeed would we all gaze in awe and the eclipse pass unnoticed.

Guided by woodcraft
Little people of the night
The cry of the loon

BETWEEN Cache Lake and Lake-of-Two-Rivers in Algonquin Park lies the Madawaska River. In some places it is wide and open, then again it narrows down so that the reeds sweep the canoe sides as you paddle along, and always it is very crooked. It is years since I first paddled down this river, and on that occasion we had planned our trip by map only. But we soon found out that whereas the map showed the Madawaska to be a crooked river, it did not show it to be nearly crooked enough. For an hour or so we paddled along. The day was far spent and the sky looked threatening. The question was, could we make Lake-of-Two-Rivers before dark and if not where could we camp on these low-lying banks?

"How far did you say it was to the next lake? It seems to me that this river goes every way except across itself, and we'll never get there," said Sid from the bow of the canoe, and I knew him well enough to detect hunger and fatigue in his voice.

"I don't know, Sid," I replied. "But I know that this river is the only way with a canoe and this outfit, unless you

want to portage down the railway track."

On we paddled. The big rocky hillside ahead drew nearer and nearer, moving from side to side as our canoe followed the bends of the river, then fell away again and dropped off into the distance behind.

Again Sid spoke. "Didn't you say you had never been over this way before?"

"Never," I replied. "Why?"

"Because I've been wondering how it is that you always steer us into the right channel. With all the bays and back reaches and blind alleys we come to you always seem to hit the river itself first thing, so that we never lose time backing out of the wrong channel and hunting for the right one."

"I have been following nature's compass," I said. "All the way along I've been watching the bottom near my paddle. If you notice in this reedy river the long blades of grass growing under water always bend in the direction of the current, no matter how slowly the river is flowing. If you come to a wide place with many bays and false channels, all you have to do is to guide the canoe down the part where the grasses all bend in the same direction, avoiding the places where they grow straight up to the surface, then you are sure you are following the right channel."

"Sounds logical to me," said Sid. "I never heard of that before. But suppose there were no weeds, what would you do?"

"Well, of course, slow-flowing rivers have weeds because they deposit silt and form soil for vegetation, and in a swift river there is no doubt of your direction. In any case, if you are puzzled about your way just stir up the mud at the bottom of the river and watch the way it flows."

Other subjects of conversation came up as we paddled along. How agreeably talk lightens labour! The river wound and turned for another hour or so, then the welcome Lake-of-Two-Rivers opened up and soon we were camped for the night.

Have you learned this little scrap of woodcraft? The next time you are pressing on to camp and the tortuous river tries your patience think of nature's guiding sign, the bending reeds in the water, and follow this unfailing indicator to the right channel. It may mean a comfortable night in camp instead of a miserable one on the river-bank.

On just such a canoe trip in the rock country of Northern Ontario, the evening meal was finished, the camp made up for the night and together we were sitting about the camp fire discussing our plans for the morrow. It was one of these clear moonless nights so typical of the northern summer. The sky was full of stars. The wind had dropped, so that a great stillness hung in the air. There did not seem to be a creature stirring.

But as the camp-fire flung its ruddy gleams about us, I noticed in its light across the smooth rock, a tiny form peeping out from beneath the moss. As it ventured farther out into the light I saw that it was a diminutive furry creature. On it came and paused a moment, blinking. Then a slight movement on my part, as I nudged my companion, made it start back and disappear into the moss. Again it appeared bringing with it another of its kind. Together they stole out little by little, until suddenly growing very bold, one snatched a crumb of the camp supper and, like a flash, both were gone again. We kept very still and, for the next few minutes, found entertanîment in the little drama these tiny creatures were acting before us. Their performance was always the same—a shy advance, a hasty nosing about, then the snatching of a morsel and a quick retreat to the friendly moss again.

As we watched them I thought of all this deep silent night was hiding away under its cloak of darkness. Here, on this few feet of rock, we had seen life and activity. There were thousands of such rocks in this land of lake and forest. Tonight we had had just one little peep behind nature's curtain of the night. We, ourselves, are creatures of the day; seeing, hearing and enjoying living nature during the hours of daylight. Yet we little think of the life which throbs about us during the hours of darkness.

Tonight we had been watching the white-footed or deer mouse. He is the most abundant and one of the prettiest of our mice. His back is pale brown and his underparts white, reminding one of the colours of the red deer. Almost at a glance we can tell his habits. Large, soft, liquid eyes, great round ears and long silky whiskers—all these can mean but one thing, a night-loving creature. Had we not seen him tonight living his life of cautious foraging, ever ready to escape?

Swift as he is, the deer mouse is not the swiftest of the mice. He may scamper over the ground, but he would be left far behind in a race with the jumping mouse. A scamper cannot keep up with a leap. The jumping mouse is also a woodland dweller that goes abroad at night. Like the deer mouse he is a little beauty. His most noticeable features are his long delicate tail, fully twice as long as his body, and a pair of well-developed hind legs.

This nimble little animal is a miniature kangaroo. Should you disturb him in the woods during the daytime, you will see only a yellow object which darts off in quick zig-zag streaks and is gone. His long tail must be a great help as a balance as he skips off.

How different both of these from the plain dull-grey meadow mouse or vole! At first glance this animal appears to be both eyeless and earless. In this it would seem that nature contradicts herself. Why has the vole not large eyes and ears as other night-loving mice? We must look more closely into his habits for the answer.

This little mouse comes out at night, true, but his wanderings are confined to following his own runways, as they wind about in the grass. He seldom strays far from these. He does not scamper about, much less hop, but toddles along his own well-beaten tracks, trusting always to his dull coat partly hidden amid the tangle of grass-blades, rather than to any speed he has, to escape enemies.

Some winter morning when you are out early for a walk you may find a little tunnel which opens out on to the smooth snow. Leading from this tunnel to another just like it is the trail of a vole traced by tiny feet. Clearly little time has been spent in the open. Well does the little rambler know that he must not linger on that dangerous white patch, he, a dark moving object on a pure white background! What if an enemy should happen to pass at that moment? The home of the timid vole is in the grassy tangle and when a runway opens out under the sky he wisely wastes no time in finding the nearest friendly grass-tuft.

And what enemies have these little foragers of the darkness? Many may be abroad seeking them as prey. If we had eyes for the night, we might see the long slender form of the weasel slink out from one of the grassy tufts. His slim lithe body seems specially built for slipping through holes. Alert, he trips along with his keen little nose to the ground. Soon he gets scent of a mouse and follows along the trail. There is but one end—a brief struggle as the weasel sinks its teeth into the living fur. The victim is devoured and the slim four-footed demon of death glides on in his hunting.

The mink, a larger and stronger animal, is abroad too. Woe unto the mouse he corners at the end of the trail! Yet there is one escape from him; he is too large to follow his prey down a small hole. Here alone lies safety from the jaws of the mink.

Overhead too there is danger. Skimming ever so silently through the air comes the keen-eyed owl, the feathered ogre of the night. Of all the enemies of the mouse-world he is most to be feared. The alert scurrying mouse may be snatched suddenly from above by silent claws that never let go.

Sometimes in the stillness of the summer night we see faint ripples on the surface of the placid lake. These tell of the little people wandering about. A strange place to wander, you think? It makes one shiver to think of spending the night swimming about in dark water. But the muskrat is as much as home in water as on land. His oily fur resists water so readily that he never gets really wet. Day and night are the same to him as he swims about. But he knows that under the cover of darkness he can work without too much wary watching. However, as long as he keeps close to his native element, the friendly water, he need only plunge beneath the surface and swim under water to his home-tunnel in the bank to outwit the foe.

I believe, of all our night prowlers, the animal that is seen least is best known. The name the beaver has made for himself is truly wonderful. Everyone knows the habits of the beaver but few have actually seen him at work. He is not often seen in daylight, much preferring to live and labour at night. Is it not true that those who toil away quietly and unseen accomplish far more than those who love to be seen and show off what they do? The humble, industrious beaver has been chosen as the national emblem of Canada, while the showy bluejay screams away unhonoured in our woods.

The beaver is indeed an industrious animal. Night after night he and his companions toil away on the community tasks, accomplishing feats that are really amazing. They are lumbermen, engineers, architects and builders. The smallest trickle of a stream is dammed up and becomes a pond. Though it may usually appear still and deserted in the gloom of a summer night, it is rippling with life as the beaver swim back and forward on their self-appointed tasks. But although their nights are very busy, the work is done for the most part in silence. The only sounds which betray the presence of beaver at work are heard when a tree, gnawed through, comes crashing down, or when some alert beaver slaps his tail upon the water as a warning of danger.

The skunk is another night prowler. He, too, has made a name for himself. But not by his works. Often the only record of his presence is the unmistakable odour which most of us know. Whenever you smell this odour you may know there is a skunk in trouble, for it is his terrible weapon of defence only. He may prowl all night nearby and you would never know that he had passed that way. I remember one evening watching a skunk only a few feet away from me hunting his supper. I followed him closely as he worked back and forth across a grassy patch and could hear his "crunch, crunch," as he chewed up some luckless beetle he caught. He knew I was there for he paused now and then to look at me. But as we were on perfectly friendly terms he had no reason to defend himself, so that his visit that evening was as harmless and odourless as though he had been a timid rabbit.

But all these are four-foots sharing the ground with us. We might almost speak of them as neighbours, though we see little of them. There is another world, above us, where bats flit and frolic. Many people do not feel kindly towards these harmless little creatures. Is it because they fly by night and so are not of our world, I wonder? Or do the ignorant imagine weird things of bats and blame them for deeds of evil? Perhaps our prejudice is because of their ugly little faces and grotesque forms. Certainly they remind one of gnomes and hobgoblins. Yet bats are but animals—we can scarcely call them four-foots—which fly remarkably well, better in fact than some birds. Naturalists tell us that the wings of bats are so sensitive that the creatures can flit swiftly through the darkness and yet in some uncanny way, feel the nearness of, and avoid, such objects as twigs and wires.

In North America we have several species of bats, but as they flutter about in the twilight these are difficult to distinguish. All are on the same errand, however, of snapping up insects in the air. If we only realized how many mosquitoes alone these little prowlers of the air devour, I am sure we would willingly forgive them their ugly looks and strange habits. After all when daylight comes the grotesque little brownies are all tucked away out of our sight in some hollow tree, their beady little eyes tightly closed in sleep.

Night is Nature's great kindly curtain which she lowers softly over her world, bringing rest to those who live and toil by day and tempting forth her creatures who love the darkness. How little we know of those who, during the hours of gloom, share the world with us! It is only when, with the return of day, we find the delicate imprint of tiny feet upon the snow or the sand, or when, as we sit by a woodland camp-fire, we peer into the darkness that we learn of the labours and frolics of these little people of the night.

A well-loved cry of the summer night plays a part in *The Northwest Passage* by Kenneth Roberts, a splendid historical novel. Its pages are full of stirring life and adventure depicting those strenuous days when the French and English struggled for the mastery of this vast continent. Quite apart from the historical romance and glamour of the story the reader cannot help admiring the skill, daring and resourcefulness of the chief character of the book, Major Rogers. Much of his success in the leadership of his famous Rangers was due not only to his tireless energy but also to his intimate knowledge of the country and its wild life. Again and again he turned his knowledge to account in his campaign against his enemies, the French and their Indian allies.

One of the most fascinating episodes in the book relates the moving of the whale-boats laden with troops up Lake Champlain. In a long line led by Rogers, the soldiers rowed stealthily through the darkness night after night, the whole expedition being concealed on shore by day. On such a silent, secret voyage no commands could be shouted, so it was agreed that the call of the loon uttered once by Rogers meant "Stop Rowing" and uttered twice, "Proceed." No better signal could have been chosen. Herein Rogers showed his skill and knowledge. The cry of this wild bird coming over the water of a still lake even during the hours of darkness was the most natural of sounds. It meant nothing to the lurking enemy scout, but was a definite order to his men in the boats.

The loon has several different cries, but Roberts, the author, does not specify which of these the resourceful major chose as his signal. Perhaps on some holiday trip on one of our northern lakes you have heard in the dead of the night a long-drawn melancholy howl that rises to a low scream and dies away again. There is something uncanny about the sound. It is almost

unbirdlike, coming as it does across the still black water. It might be the voice of any wild creature, real or imagined, and were you not familiar with the wild life of the north it would strike terror into your being, the terror of the unknown. Yet this eerie note is simply the call of the loon to its kind. It was most likely this cry that Major Rogers used to his troops on those dark nights long ago on Lake Champlain. It is easily imitated and has great carrying power.

Paddling your canoe across the lake some summer day you may pass a couple of loons. As you look at these graceful voyagers swimming strongly against the waves, you see that they are watching you. The sun gleams on their long pointed bills as they turn their heads this way and that in eyeing your movements. Then one of them opens his bill and utters a short quavering laugh, a note that sounds both questioning and suspicious. Then in a twinkling both birds have plunged beneath the waves and there is no telling when or where they will reappear on the surface.

Though a strong swimmer and a skilful diver, the loon is also a powerful bird on the wing. Often he is seen travelling swiftly overhead, high above the tops of the forest trees, bound for some distant lake. With his long bill and outstretched neck and his feet behind him he is easily recognized. As his great wings drive him through the air like a huge arrow, his loud, long, tremulous call may be heard over and over again. This call is much the same note as the laugh of the loon on the lake, but louder and greatly prolonged. Anyone knowing the habits of the loon can distinguish at once these two calls, the one of the flying and the one of the swimming loon.

The strangest and wildest of his cries is an ear-splitting scream of two bars, the first rising from a low note to a high shrill pitch, then dropping again to a low ending. This is repeated several times as the bird throws its head violently back and forward. The wolf-like howl referred to above may sound uncanny but this is really terrifying. It is unlike the voice of any other living creature and quite unlike what is usually associated with bird-music. Yet it is possible that this unearthly scream may be the love-song of the loon, for it is often heard in spring and when several loons are together.

One spring when on a canoe trip in the northland I was standing on a rocky point idly watching a pair of loons through the field-glasses. One of them was acting in a very unusual manner. He—surely the male—was swimming back and forth rapidly before the other sending the water flying up before him in a way that suggested great glee. Then he would pause before the other and utter a soft cooing note, a note fitted only to express the tenderest emotions. Perhaps there is a time in the life of even this strange bird of primitive habits and uncouth voice when it yields to the all-powerful influence of love. Surely then this low soft call must be the true love-song of the loon.

Wings in the dusk
Bat and flying squirrel

Ramble eight

THERE are two birds belonging to the same family, which look much alike, but the more we speak about them the more different we find they are in many respects. And although they are closely related I doubt if they ever see each other. One is badly named—we ourselves named it. The other is well named—it has named itself. One is often seen and heard. The other is often heard and seldom seen. What birds are they? Well, if you haven't already guessed I'll tell you. The nighthawk and the whippoorwill.

I believe everyone living in either the country or the city whether interested in bird life or not, knows the nighthawk. He is one of these fellows who loves to make a big noise. We all know people like that, don't we? Generally they are harmless. The nighthawk in spite of his sinister name is quite harmless. He often flies about by day and he isn't a hawk at all. So, as I have said, he is badly named. If you have never seen a nighthawk at close quarters, let me describe him. He is about ten inches long and with such long wings that from tip to tip they extend some twenty inches. These wings are pointed and each has a large white spot on the quills which is easily seen from below as he flies.

Now when a bird has long pointed wings you know at once that it must be a strong flier. The next thing we notice is the tail of the nighthawk. It is decidedly forked and serves as a good rudder. His feet are very small and weak. A true hawk would have strong feet and sharp claws. His head is large and round with a very small bill, but a tremendously large gape. When a nighthawk opens his bill it seems as though the whole top of his head opens like a lid. His eyes too are very large.

Now a naturalist on examining a nighthawk would say: "Long pointed wings, forked tail, small feet, small bill but with a wide gape, and large eyes—this bird flies a great deal, mostly at night, and feeds upon insects which it catches while in flight."

Almost any evening during the months of May and June in towns, and even in large cities, you can look up into the air and see this strange bird. He will be flitting about in a loose straggling flight that takes him higher and higher in the air. All this time he utters a harsh nasal note, which is written in bird books as "Pe-ent." Sometimes he takes a lunge to one side; this means he has caught some passing insect. It may be a fly, a gnat, a moth or even a

June bug. Whatever it is, he seldom misses for his mouth is very wide. So, perhaps after all he *is* really a hawk—to the insects.

After attaining a good height he pauses in his erratic flight, poises a moment, then drops headlong to earth. Down, down he comes swifter and swifter in a reckless dash as though he would plunge into some roof-top. But no. At the last moment he turns and glides upward in a graceful curve. At that moment we hear a deep, loud humming whirr. This sound is not made vocally, but by the air rushing through the stiff wing feathers. The bird seems to realize he hasn't a musical voice, so he plays an instrument. And, how he enjoys playing it! Again and again he goes through this manœuvre, as though rejoicing in the thought that many eyes may be watching him from below.

If he is thus busy hunting and booming all night, when does he sleep? Often in broad daylight and wherever he happens to find himself—on a roof, chimney, or on the bare ground. So well does his mottled plumage match the surroundings that a nighthawk at rest is a difficult thing to see. What a carefree existence, feeding on the wing and resting anywhere! This would lead you to think that the nighthawk has no home. This is literally true. The female builds no nest but simply deposits her eggs on a bare patch of ground and brings up her babies without the slightest pretence of a nest. There might be a nighthawk "nesting," if I may use the term, on the roof of your home right now. If so you will find two mottled eggs or two downy young but no nest. So we might say that the young nighthawks are brought up out in the wide world and never know a home.

So much for the nighthawk.

His cousin the whippoorwill lives in the country and never comes to the city. As I have said he has named himself. I suppose everyone has heard him calling from the woods. "Whippoorwill, whippoorwill, whippoorwill," he calls over and over again in a monotonous refrain. Though often heard, he is seldom seen. In appearance he resembles his relative, the nighthawk. His eyes are large, his bill is small, he has a very wide gape fringed with long stiff bristles. He has long wings and a broad fan-shaped tail, not forked as is the tail of the nighthawk. You see the whippoorwill flits softly through the deep, dark forest at night so this broad tail must help him wonderfully as he glides along catching insects. He does not dart from side to side as his city relative. And should he miss a moth, the fringe of bristles at the side of his mouth catches it and with one sweep of his foot he pushes it into his mouth.

On several occasions I have had a whippoorwill respond to even my poor imitation of his note. I recall one cool September evening a number of us had gathered around a camp-fire in a secluded valley to enjoy a cornroast. One after another, as called upon, we told some camp-fire yarn. I had been asked to tell about some of

our birds. I had mentioned the whippoorwill and by way of illustration I whistled an imitation of his well-known refrain. To everyone's surprise, including my own, from the nearby shrubbery in response came the chant of a real whippoorwill. Not the clear ringing notes we hear in the flush of spring song season, but a hushed subdued reply, but none the less thrilling to those present.

Another experience I shall always recall with pleasure was one summer evening while on a motor trip. We had driven down a long, wild, overgrown road which brought us to the shore of a lake. Here in a little poplar bluff we parked our car and prepared to spend the night.

It was a beautiful evening. Before us stretched the blue water with its green shore opposite, all looking so much bluer and greener in the rich glow of the sloping rays of the setting sun. The sandpiper was calling from the water's edge. The white-throat and the hermit thrush sang from the nearby woods. Except for bird music there was everywhere that quiet hush found only where all is as nature made it. How good that wood fire smelled as we cooked our evening meal! And how contentedly we settled down in our blankets for the night!

As dusk closed in all around, suddenly from just outside the tent came the loud ringing refrain of the whippoorwill. Then another a little farther away, and another still more distant. We had made our camp amidst a colony of these musicians of the night. I put my head outside the tent door and whistled an imitation of their notes. Instantly I saw a shadowy form flit through the dusk and settle on the stones of our fire-place. And the next moment there came the familiar bars: "Whippoorwill, whippoorwill, whippoorwill." Again I whistled and the bird flew straight for me and settled on the roof of the tent a few inches above my head. Once more I replied and in the dim light I saw his form fly over and come to rest on the roof of our car where he sang his refrain again and again.

I have often wondered what was in that bird's mind as he flitted about vainly seeking the elusive voice so close at hand. Was it mere curiousity? Was he jealous of intrusion? Or did he hope to find a companion? Whatever it may have been I, on my part, know what I was thinking. I was wondering how many people while on a motor trip, have the thrill of seeing a whippoorwill settle and chant from their tent and from the roof of their car a few feet away.

But did you ever have an unexpected midnight visitor? One that came uninvited, made his presence felt in a strange uncanny way and departed silently, leaving you wondering vaguely if the visit had really taken place or not.

Twice during one month I had such visitors. The first time I awoke in the dead of the night with a feeling that there was something unusual in the room. I could see nothing and yet from time to time I felt something pass near me in the darkness and thought I could hear a quiet fluttering sound. I knew there was nothing to be afraid of and yet I was puzzled.

Then, all at once the mystery was explained. A large bat fluttered against the screen that was stretched across the open window and clung to the netting with outstretched wings. Here it paused long enough for me to see its shape clearly silhouetted against the dim light outside. Then it climbed up the netting to the space at the top and vanished into the night. So, after all there was nothing uncanny or even mysterious about the visitation. Simply that a bat in the course of its flight had found its way in, and could not get out again so easily.

I suppose if I had been living several generations ago, such an experience would have been considered the fore-runner of great misfortune. To have such an ill-omened beast hover about one's bed in the dead of night would have foreboded almost any ill luck. For some reason, man in the past has had a great dread of bats. Even today, with many people, that antipathy still exists. We hear the strangest stories about bats, even to the effect that they bring bedbugs into the home and that they get into one's hair.

As a matter of fact bats are harmless, innocent creatures in the world of nature, and not nearly so much to be feared as many smaller things that fly by night. I would far rather know that there were many bats about my bed than a few mosquitos. For with the coming of the bats the mosquitos disappear.

The bat has been described in a casual way as "a mouse with wings." But one glance at the two animals reveals obvious differences. In fact the only similarity is that both animals have short close fur. Imagine the two tiny front feet of a mouse greatly lengthened until they resemble arms, and you at once have one great difference in structure between the bat and the mouse. Now, imagine a thin delicate membrane of skin stretched from the greatly lengthened first finger of one hand to all the other long fingers in turn, joining up both hind feet and the tail, right around to the fingers of the other hand. In short the bat is surrounded from one hand to the other by this membrane which connects all the fingers, both feet, and its tail. This membrane becomes a pair of wings when the bat chooses to fly.

And what wings they are! We are much inclined to think of birds as blessed above all other creatures with powers of flight. True, birds are wonderful fliers. And many insects are very skilful on the wing. But some birds are not able to fly at all. The ostrich, the emu and the apteryx are all flightless birds. But nature seems to have singled out the bat of all fur-bearing (I nearly said four-footed) animals and endowed it with rare ability in the air. Strange as it may seem, bats fly much more skilfully than do ducks, geese, owls and many marsh birds, and perhaps every bit as well as many of our smaller song birds. We are apt to doubt this as we watch the first bat visible in the fading light of evening. It flutters about like a great lumbering butterfly. But if we only had eyes to pierce the gloom of night and to follow a bat as it sails and sweeps, wheels and darts this way and that, when this voyager of the darkness gets down to business, we would be inclined to give birds second place as fliers after all.

Though we might readily describe a bat as a "fly-by-night," do not imagine that his deeds are evil. Those whirling fantastic curves through the night air are not performed for the mere joy of flying. Bats feed almost entirely on insects. And if we realized the number of insects, especially mosquitoes, devoured during a summer night, we would count these curious little animals among our best friends.

Why, then, are bats so much dreaded and misunderstood? Frankly I believe it is because people do not know much about them. We are all prone to fear what we do not understand. And from the beginning of history man has had an instinctive dread of darkness, and consequently of creatures that prowl by night. Little wonder then that the harmless, yes, beneficial, bat comes in for its share of prejudice.

There is another more cogent reason, for I believe in all nature's world there are no creatures so ugly as bats. I am familiar with several species which occur about my home, and when I think of them all with their quaint little faces, great long loose ears, little black upturned pug noses, widely grinning mouths and tiny beady eyes—every one of them looking like a little evil hobgoblin in its ugliness—I am tempted to say, "Well, your deeds may be ever so good; but you are certainly the homeliest family I ever knew." Of course nobody likes ugliness or ugly things, and when we associate their looks with their uncanny habits of the dark, we can hardly wonder that these innocent little friends of man have become creatures of ill-omen to the uninformed.

There is one villain in this much-maligned family, however, the vampire bat. This dreaded species has the grim habit of sucking the blood of other animals and of people while they sleep. So insidiously is this done that the victims do not awake. The vampire derives its name from the curious European legend or superstition of a corpse which arises from the grave and wanders forth at night to suck the blood of former friends. As this unholy bat inhabits the tropics we have nothing to fear from it in North America.

My other midnight visitor came in much the same manner. I was sleeping on a screened porch at a cottage in the north surrounded by woods. The moon had risen like a great yellow ball over the trees in the east. Night had closed in and I had drifted off to sleep to the monotonous chant of the whippoorwills and the gentle trilling of the screech owl.

At some time during the hours of darkness, I was awakened by the sound of little feet hurrying across the roof of the porch, and a moment later I heard the gentle "plop" of something striking against the screen, making it hum a low musical note. I looked out and on the netting against the dim sky I saw clinging to the meshes a broad, flat, four-footed creature with a long wide tail. It was but the work of a moment to pick up the flash-light and throw a beam upon this midnight visitor. As he remained motionless in the light I could see two large bright black eyes gazing at me, two big velvety ears, and a delicate little nose set with rows of long silky whiskers. Of course I knew my visitor at once. There was no mistaking those eyes and ears and that downy fur with a broad tail. It was a flying squirrel.

For some time he clung to the netting blinking in the light, then he sprang off and was gone into the night. It was as though he had intruded his presence into my dreams for a brief instant and then was swallowed up in the darkness.

The flying squirrel has many relatives, all better known than he. Everyone is familiar with the red squirrel, the tawny little rascal found in almost every woodlot. Being diurnal in his habits, noisy and active, he has made himself perhaps the best known of

all our smaller animals. Winter and summer he is abroad, for we find his tracks on the snow as often as we see him aloft in the leafy branches.

Another member of the family is the chipmunk, or better described as the striped squirrel. This is the smallest of the family and, to my mind, the prettiest. His brown coat is conspicuously marked by a series of buff and black stripes. A stump fence or rock pile is his favourite haunt. He seldom ventures aloft, preferring the security of the crannies. Sometimes you may be tempted into the woods to discover the source of an oft-repeated note—"Coo, coo, coo"—and find it to be a chipmunk, seated upon a stump. At your approach he at once dives into some retreat at the roots of his stump-castle. The baron of the fortress breathing out defiance seeks safety in flight at the sight of the foe. Of late years there has been a great increase in the number of black and grey squirrels in our towns and cities. Though it is not generally known, these are both the same species. The normal colour is grey, but for some reason, not thoroughly understood, certain individuals become quite black and pass as a different species. For years this squirrel was a rarity, but due to protection it has multiplied and is now frequently seen dodging motors on city streets. Probably more squirrels than pedestrians are run down.

These are the relatives of the flying squirrel. In a general way they are much alike—having close tight fur and long bushy tails, and being busy, active little creatures of diurnal habits. But nature delights in exceptions. In this interesting family she has one unique member. While all his brethren are abroad in daylight, the flying squirrel is dozing in some hollow tree. And when the shades of night gather and his day-loving neighbours cease their scamperings, this owl among the squirrels sallies forth for a night of foraging. His food consists of nuts, seeds, buds and fruit in season. And whereas his relatives must be ever on the look-out for hawks, he, on his part, must beware of owls, as he scrambles and sails about.

Nature has equipped him in a wonderful way for his night-prowling. He has large delicate eyes, ample ears and long sensitive whiskers. All these must be of great use to him amid the darkness. But above all she has blessed him with the power of flight. Of course he cannot fly with the same skill as the bat. In fact, the flying squirrel does not fly at all. His broad flat body and flat tail are greatly accentuated by a web of furry skin which is stretched along his flanks. So that the little creature merely springs into the air and, if I may use the term, "spreads himself" and in the lightest, airiest way floats through space for many yards and makes a perfect "four-point landing" on any chosen spot.

Comparisons are odious, I know, but they are also interesting. Twice during one month I had been awakened, as related, by midnight visitors, but how different those visitors! The bat blundering into the room with his stealthy, fluttering flight, settling for a moment to show his uncanny black filmy wings and ugly little visage, like an evil little sprite of the darkness, and then vanishing into the night. And the gentle lovable flying squirrel, clad in the softest of fawn-coloured fur, pausing to gaze mildly at me with its big bright eyes and then to skim away in the gloom.

Plants that eat insects
Children of the sand

Ramble nine

One summer holiday I spent part of my time in a swamp. That does not sound like very much fun, I know. One would hardly choose a swamp as a place to have a picnic. Even the very word makes us think of a wet, boggy, soggy spot where there is no place to sit down. Well, perhaps it is but then I was not there on a picnic. I went in to find certain plants which I knew grew nowhere else. As you know, plants are like all other things in nature, they are found where they belong. So, if you know your plants well, you know just where to find them and when.

This swamp was really a beautiful natural garden. There were graceful waving grasses and sedges, some with hard prickly heads, like the giants' clubs we read about in fairy tales, others like the cotton grass which, as though in contrast to giant clubs, is a tassel of soft white wool. There were broad patches of marsh marigold, then in seed, and large bunches of pink and white cranberry flowers. Trailing about, crossing and recrossing themselves, were the long stems of the twin flower with its pair of bells, mingled with the goldthread whose rootlets are as strands of golden wire. And here and there above these stood out the most beautiful of all wild flowers, the pink mocassin flower and the yellow lady's slipper.

Over all arched tall cedars, spruces and tamaracs shading this garden below, keeping it cool from the blazing sun which otherwise would have killed the delicate plant life on the ground. There were many interesting things to see and examine, but I want to tell you of two which attracted me and for which I had come to this swamp especially.

The first was the pitcher plant. It is the strangest-looking plant you can imagine. It has several tall slim stems growing up from a broad circle of leaves. These stems have at their summits a large single flower about three inches across. These flowers are composed of many parts. First there are the five green sepals as they are called. Then five bright purple petals, rounded and ample. Over these is a large five-pointed shield or canopy, which more or less shades the petals and under which grow the stamens. I know of several plants which hold their leaves spread out above the flowers like an umbrella; but this is the only one I know of having an umbrella *on* its flower. I can't quite see the idea myself, but then the plant is not asking my opinion.

It is the leaves growing around the stem which I am going to tell you about. These are different in shape from the leaves of any other plant. Instead of being broad and flat they are round and hollow like a jug. Down the back is a keel-shaped ridge which resembles the handle and at the mouth there is a broad open curved lip. Into the open hollow part of this leaf the rain water runs and remains below as a pool. You can pick up the leaf by its ridge-shaped handle and pour this water out of it just as you would pour water out of a jug. It is the curious shape of these leaves that gives the plant the name of pitcher plant.

But there is a real purpose in these odd-shaped leaves. If we look closely at the lip of the "pitcher" we find it is not smooth as elsewhere on the leaf but thickly set with tiny hairs all pointing *downwards*. A bug or caterpillar crawling along the leaf and on to the lip finds it very easy to crawl downward. So the silly insect rambles on over the tiny hairs, down, down until at length far below in his crawling he comes to the pool of water inside the pitcher-shaped leaf. Farther he cannot go, so he turns to crawl out. But there is no *out*. The moment he turns he finds all the tiny hairs arrayed against him like so many bayonets. No matter how he struggles he cannot gain a step. At last, exhausted, he drops into the pool where he drowns and sinks to the bottom. Here his decomposing corpse is absorbed little by little by the plant as food.

So this strange inhabitant of the swamp actually captures its insect prey and devours it.

Another interesting thing about the pitcher plant is its name. You know every plant and creature in nature has at least two names. One by which we ordinary folks know it and another—its scientific name—known only to really learned people. For instance, we speak of the plant just described as the "Pitcher Plant." It is also called "Huntsman's Cap." But scientists have named it "Sarracenia." It is not often I mention scientific names because they can make an interesting study very dry. But this name and its origin adds a delightful little historical touch to our pitcher plant's story.

Early in the seventeen-hundreds, when the French ruled Canada and were having a difficult time trying to rule the Indians, there was a French doctor named Sarracen living at Quebec. Apparently he did not have much to occupy his time, so he used to take rambles off into the woods. On one of these rambles he found this strange plant, our pitcher plant of today. (Plants do not change in two or three centuries. They are not like cars, having new models every so often.) Its jug-shaped leaves interested the doctor greatly. So he took some specimens with him on his next trip home to France. I should have liked to hear some of the stories he told about Canada, of the Indians, and other strange things he found here. One story at least he could verify by showing the actual specimen. Well, the French scientists were so impressed that they named the plant after this doctor. So really the pitcher plant has done more for the doctor than he ever did for it. For, were it not for its scientific name, who today would know that the good Doctor Sarracen ever lived?

The other plant I found which I would like to tell you of is the sun-dew. This is a tiny plant that grows where it is quite wet, raising its stalk some six inches above the soil. On this stalk there

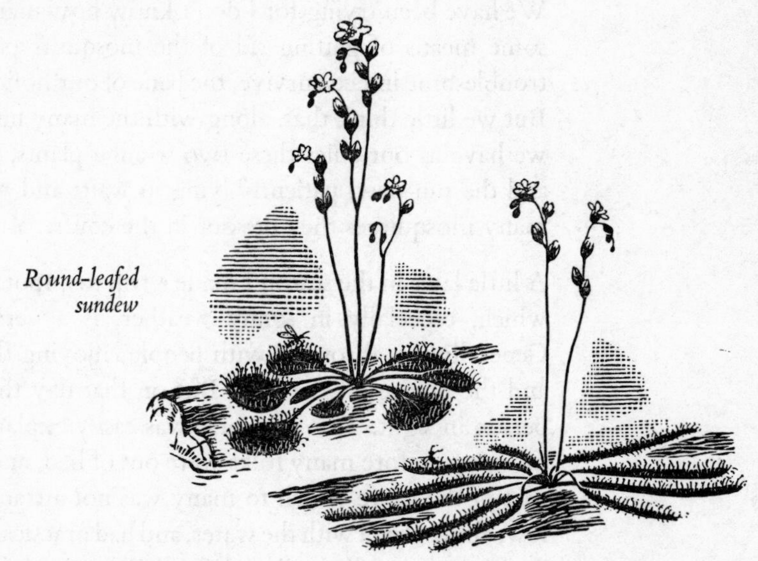

Round-leafed sundew

Long-leafed sundew

are several little white flowers, and around it grows a rosette of leaves flat on the ground. Again the leaves interest us. Each is covered with little hairs and each hair is tipped with sticky nectar, hence the name sun-dew.

Just imagine what a tempting object that little leaf must be to a passing fly! Attracted by the glitter he is sure to alight upon the leaf. In a twinkling he is seized and held by the sticky nectar. Of course he struggles and strange to say all the little hairs nearby bend over and lend a hand in entangling the hapless insect. So before long he is all gummed up. Perhaps this is where we ourselves got the idea of sticky fly-paper for that pest, the house fly. At last he is borne down upon the surface of the leaf. Then the real horror begins. The leaf exudes a juice and the helpless captive is digested alive.

The pitcher plant allows the insect to climb upon its leaf and helps it downward and humanely drowns its prey before devouring it. But this little imp, the sun-dew, actually tempts the unsuspecting fly to its doom and devours it alive.

I could feel little sympathy, though, for the victims. All the time I was in the swamp I was continually slapping mosquitoes. They were everywhere. Their ceaseless hum was distracting and their stinging almost unendurable. This was the one thing that marred my pleasure throughout the afternoon.

We have been trying for I don't know how many years to devise some means of getting rid of the mosquito pest, and still the troublesome insects survive, the bane of our holidays in the north. But we little think that, along with the many insectivorous birds, we have as our allies these two strange plants, the pitcher plant and the sun-dew, patiently lying in wait; and who can tell how many mosquitoes they devour in the course of a season?

A little later in the season I made a trip to a spot on the lake shore which, especially in sunny weather, is a very inviting place. Generally it is thronged with people enjoying the sun, the water and the breeze off the lake. But on that day there was hardly a person in sight. This of course was easily explained. It was early morning, before many folks were out of bed, and I had come to a part of the shore which to many was not attractive. It was quite low, almost level with the water, and had practically no vegetation. Such a spot is called a "mud-flat." That certainly does not sound like a place to go for pleasure. But to the naturalist, no nook or cranny, however uninviting, is neglected or overlooked in his search for information. There is no telling what secrets lurk in the oddest corners, or what will be found in the most out-of-the-way spots. The marsh, the swamp, the mud-flat—only the naturalist knows their treasures.

At first when I approached this mud-flat it seemed quite devoid of life of any sort. But as I drew nearer I found it to be teeming with bird life. There were two or three kinds of plover, several different sandpipers and one or two kindred shore birds often seen with these.

There is something fascinating about finding a group of interesting birds so unexpectedly. It was though they had come into existence by magic. The sordid mud-flat suddenly revealed a flock of dainty birds. They all appeared very busy. Some were standing still preening their plumage. Some were bathing, sending the water flying and making the little ripples ooze out from them. Others were picking their way about with mincing little steps searching for morsels of food. Occasionally two saw the same morsel and a tussle followed. At my approach many ran several yards and then stood still watching me.

Whatever they were doing they were difficult to see. Had I been asked to tell the exact number of birds in any given area I could not have done so with certainty. Even a slight movement on the part of the flock revealed birds unseen before.

You might wonder why there should be any difficulty in seeing birds so decidedly marked, especially out in the open without cover. Shore birds with mottled backs and white breasts one would think ought to stand out against a plain background of mud. But here we find a good example of nature's subtlest touch in the art of concealment. It is well known that many birds and animals have colour-patterns or are coloured in such a way as to render them almost invisible on the background of their natural habitats. Good examples are the mottled plumage of the partridge in the woods and the streaked feathers of the snipe in the grass. But shore birds with their light breasts seem to set at nought this law. Yet it has been found that actually the colour-pattern of these children of the sands, dark above and light below as it is, in a wonderful way is neutralised by the strong light above and the shade below, so that the birds are difficult, if not impossible, to see. It is not surprising, then, that as I approached the mud-flat it appeared lifeless though many birds were there.

One of the first I noticed was the killdeer plover. I might have known he would be there, for he is the commonest of our plovers. As early in spring as March we see him winging his way across the sky calling "Kill-deer, kill-deer." He has been named after his call. As I looked at this handsome plover I could not help wondering at his strange markings. Around his neck is a broad collar of black and another of white, then a second band of black on his breast. His head too is similarly marked. With such contrasting colours one would expect him to be seen afar. Yet, strange to say, this very arrangement of colours blends into the surroundings so perfectly that the actual outline of the bird is lost to the eye.

I never had this fact so well demonstrated as one day when I was walking along this very beach. Some distance off I noticed a flock of killdeers. At first I thought there were perhaps a dozen birds. I looked them over through my field-glasses, and found there were as many as twenty. But the longer I looked at the group the less certain I could be of their number. The checkered effect of so many bands of black and white on the many heads, necks and breasts as the birds moved about was too confusing for the eye. There is no better example of the application of this curious method of concealment in the affairs of man than during the days of the first world war. We recall how the ships on the high seas were painted not plain blue-grey like their ocean background, but banded in the most fantastic patterns or "dazzled" as it was called. The result of such a pattern was, as one seaman told me expressively, "You don't know whether you are looking at one ship or three." So with this flock of "dazzled" plover, I did not know whether I was looking at twelve birds or twenty.

With the killdeer I found another plover. He is a smaller edition, for his colour-pattern follows closely that of the larger bird. In fact the ring around his neck has suggested his name, ring or semipalmated plover. It would seem that this system of coloration is a very successful scheme for concealment. It is on such beaches as this that we find the similarly banded piping plover also. To me the plaintive notes of this little bird recall broad open beaches of rippled ochre sand. I hear the swish and roar of the nearby waves, but above this sound, so deep and resonant, comes the sweet mellow whistle of the piping plover and I see his tiny form running swiftly across the level beach. Then, as the bird halts, he is instantly lost to view, melting as it were, into the drab background of ochre sand.

Plovers always seem to me to be very serious birds. They move about sedately and often stand for a long time on one leg as though in deep thought. They quite lack the carefree, sociable nature of the sandpipers. Even their calls are plaintive; the note of the killdeer has a distressed tone. The sandpipers, on the other hand, thoroughly enjoy their life on the beach with its wind-driven breakers curling in to thunder on the smooth shining sand.

That morning it was interesting to watch the several kinds of sandpipers as they sported about, feeding, preening themselves and tussling together. The spotted sandpiper was there, although in many cases he was in fall plumage without distinctive spots. It might have been difficult to recognize him thus clad, but for his irrepressible habit of bobbing and teetering whenever he tries to stand still. With him was his larger cousin, the solitary sandpiper, though why "solitary" I cannot say, for here he was as sociable as any of them.

This bird has a very interesting chapter in his life history. For many years his nesting habits were a mystery. No naturalist had ever found the bird's nest. Perhaps all searched in the wrong place —on the ground, where one would naturally look for the nest of a shore bird. At length it was discovered that this long-legged wader actually nests in trees, often in the deserted nests of such birds as the grackle or the robin.

No group of shore birds would be complete without the dainty little sanderlings. These, of all our beach-loving birds, are the true children of the sands. Their name is most aptly applied. One of the prettiest sights one could wish to see is a long stretch of clean sandy beach with its ever-changing surf line, and on it a little group of sanderlings running nimbly up and down the gleaming sand, advancing and retreating as the waves sweep up and down the smooth beach, snatching a morsel of food here and there. Then suddenly as though in response to a given signal, the whole flock springs into the air and is gone, leaving the beach strangely deserted.

And as though by way of contrast, the tall, graceful sandpiper known as the yellowlegs was here. I say by contrast because I think this bird is as prosaicly named as the sanderling is aptly. Yet certainly the first thing one notices about him is his long, bright yellow legs. It almost looks as though he had donned a pair of high rubber boots of that bright hue to wade about, for he often goes right into the water up to his "hips."

As I expected, I found in this little group that morning a strange wader which is neither plover nor sandpiper—the turnstone. He is an interesting fellow, having the habits of both of these waders and some of his own. He has a curious way of running along the shore and, while other waders are content to let things turn up, seeing to it that things turn up for him.

Every pebble he comes upon he gives a flip with his bill, making it roll away. Often as a reward he finds some morsel of food underneath it. It is amusing to watch this little beachcomber toddling along the sand, sending the pebbles rolling this way and that. His must be a profitable method of hunting for the turnstone has been at it for a long time, and I suppose he will always hunt this way. What puzzles me, however, is that no other shore-bird has acquired the same habit. Surely they all see the turnstone at work!

But why this gathering of shore-birds? What is in the mind of the sandpiper, the plover and the turnstone as they meet here? Food and each others' company? Possibly. But there is a far deeper urge. As yet it is only late summer, but already they feel that it is time for them to be off south. This gathering of the waders is the first sign we see of that great southward journey made by myriads of our birds over all the land. Some of these I saw on the mud-flat that day had come down from their northern homes on the barren grounds. They would linger with us a short while, then, one by one or in small companies, move onward, pausing to rest and feed at one mud-flat after another which they have learned are there to harbour them, until at last these children of the sands will arrive at their homes in far-off foreign climes.

The spider's masterpiece
Birds not of a feather

THERE is a story told of a political prisoner who spent the long lonely hours in tossing five pins to the far end of his dimly lighted cell and finding them again. Once I was a prisoner for some weeks, confined to my room as the result of an accident. Like the political prisoner I found time hanging heavy on my hands. I did many things but each in turn became tiresome. One day I happened to notice just outside my window a fine large garden spider in his web. Now, I thought, I am going to have something interesting to watch.

Everyone is familiar with the web of the garden spider, but how many have seen him weave his wonderful structure? It is considered by naturalists to be one of the wonders of the insect world—though to be strictly accurate, spiders are not insects; they are more nearly related to crabs.

When I first noticed this web at my window it was somewhat damaged. But the following morning the whole structure was completely replaced by a new and perfect web. Clearly the spider worked at night and lay in wait during the day, either in the web

or in some hidden retreat among the leaves of the Boston ivy vine around the window.

So after dark I let the reading lamp shine out of the window, and there he was preparing to renew his net for the night's catch. There was already one very strong strand of web stretched across the window from leaf to leaf of the ivy vine that clung to the bricks. It bridged the gap and formed the key line or main guy of the whole web. Along this the spider ran leisurely and, after fastening a new strand to an ivy leaf, he dropped down and fastened the other end to the window below. Next minute he was scrambling up this new line again, aloft to the main guy. From this he dropped another upright line to the window sill at another point. This operation he repeated several times from one line to another at various points till he built an angled framework enclosing an opening about ten inches across. Every little while, in doing all this, he came upon some of the damaged remains of yesterday's web. These he simply nipped off and let them float away freely.

Now the framework was finished, irregular in shape and outline, but very strong. This was the first stage. One would think that the industrious little toiler would pause and rest and consider what would be the best way to proceed. It seemed to me that he must be very tired clinging on to almost invisible lines of web with the delicate hold of such spindly legs. But not he! Without a moment's hesitation, and with the air of one who knows exactly what he intends to do, he strung a line straight across the open framework from side to side. Along this he ran, and at another point he fastened a second line like the first across the opening. Then a third, and a fourth, and so on, till the whole opening was criss-crossed with lines, all radiating from about the centre so that the whole structure now looked like the spokes of a wheel with the hub in the middle. Thus the second stage was completed and the web began to take shape.

Again one would imagine the spider would rest from what seemed such tiring work. But no. At once he began to weave in the spiral lines which extend from spoke to spoke, making the typical cobweb appearance we all know so well. Working from

the hub outward, he went around and around laying the spiral line on each spoke till at last he came to the outer framework. Here he stopped. The web now looked perfect and complete to my eyes, but I learned there was still another stage to go through. As he worked I saw that this was the most important of all.

Beginning now where he was, at the outer edge of the web, the painstaking little worker laid a second spiral line from spoke to spoke parallel to the first, but in every space he laid two new strands. As he laid these last strands from point to point I saw at once that they were of a different kind of web from all previously used. The frame, the spokes, and the first spiral were all woven of a thin strong dry web stretched tightly in place. This last spiral was not only very sticky but quite elastic. It was this strand that really caught the insect prey. The fly that flew into the web stuck to this strand and in its struggles the strand stretched so that the hapless insect could not help becoming entangled in other nearby sticky strands. This I found out by touching the web. All other lines were dry, but this last spiral stuck to my finger and stretched four times its length before it broke away.

The instant I touched the web the spider halted in his work, ran to the central hub, where he tried all the spokes to learn which one had brought in the message. But it was a false alarm. No fly was in the web. He shook it vigorously to be sure, waited a moment longer, then returned to his work where he had left off. Around and around he went, leaving the delicate sticky web behind him firmly attached at each point where it crossed the spokes. On and on he worked and, try as I might, I could not follow the operation of his eight spindly legs. He seemed to know just where to put each leg and how to pull each silken strand taut and in place and fasten it, without thought or pause. He worked like a little spinning machine, simply scrambling nimbly along those almost invisible lines, and the web grew in pattern before my eyes.

At last he arrived at the hub again and settled himself head downward to await whatever prey chance might bring. The web was complete. In less than half an hour this patient, adroit, humble little toiler had, without a lesson, without tools, and without help, planned, spun and completed one of the most intricate, beautiful structures in nature. And to-morrow he would do so all over again. I could not but marvel at his untutored skill. Nor could I help wondering how long it would have taken the most skilled workman, with the most delicate sense of touch, given all the tools he required and all the time he asked, to create such a masterpiece.

For several weeks my friend the spider was there. He earned his living as nature had taught him. But he little knew the entertainment he gave me, confined as I was to my room. It certainly was more fun to watch him weave his wonderful web than to toss pins about to find them over and over again.

Just outside a studio from which I broadcast sometimes there is a smooth, level lawn. On two sides there are buildings, on the third side a streetcar yard, and at the end a tennis court, so that the lawn is really the only bit of nature in the whole square—and it is man-made. As I drove away from the studio one evening, I happened to see several birds feeding on this lawn. It was a pretty sight. The sun was low in the west. His long sloping rays lighted up the green grass vividly. And though there was a tennis game in progress and plenty of traffic roaring along the public street beyond, and buildings all about, this little touch of nature amid such surroundings was refreshing to say the least.

I stopped to look over the birds (for you never can tell when you may see something interesting), and at once noticed that there were four different kinds on this lawn—robins, several sparrows, a number of starlings and one flicker.

Now there is nothing unusual about seeing any of these birds in the city. Almost any city lawn may have two or even three of them upon it. But it is not often you will see four in the same place at the same time. These four kinds of birds were not of the same feather, not even of the same family. But all had gathered here for the same purpose of finding something to eat. As I watched them it occurred to me that the most noticeable thing about these birds was not that they were different, but that they were so very different in so many ways—in plumage, in size, in actions, in mannerisms, and in the way in which each found its food. In fact, the longer I watched them the less they seemed to have in common. And they seemed to know it, for no one of them paid a bit of attention to the other even when close together.

Take the robin, for example. He is plump and a fair size with a black head and, as we all know, a fine red breast. He was the most dignified one of the group. He held himself erect and stood very still. Then he ran (not hopped or walked) a few yards very quickly, stopped, stood still again, then lowered his head and gave the ground at his feet very close attention. He seemed to be watching and listening at once. Suddenly he went to work vigorously and unearthed a worm. This he drew out gently, firmly and so skilfully that he got the worm out whole, swallowed it and ran on to another place, where he posed with dignity again. He seemed to be the gentleman, the aristocrat of the group.

Undoubtedly he was. The robin belongs to the thrush family, and the thrushes are, of all our birds, the most gifted and the most blessed with the little refinements which nature can bestow. All the thrush family are good singers. I need only mention the names of some of the members and nature-lovers will recall their voices —the bluebird with his soft warbling, the wood thrush singing his silvery bell-like notes in the forest glen, the weird strains of the veery in the evening hush, and that gifted musician of the northern woods, the hermit thrush. The robin is no mean songster among them. His cheerful warble is one of the first of our bird songs heard in the spring. The beauty of the robin's song is that it is one of the familiar bird carols heard in the city. No matter how few bird's voices city folks may know, I doubt if there is a city dweller any place who does not know the song of the robin.

I sometimes think that nature must have been in a kindly mood when she sent this large, handsome, red-breasted thrush to live right in the city with us. And how well he fits into urban life! He finds his food of worms on the lawns of the city parks. His nest of mud and grasses is built on a veranda post or window ledge. The mother robin feeds her young right before our eyes and it is no rare thing for any of us who walk city streets to hear, amid the roar of the traffic, the strains of a robin's song. The robin is a native of this country. The early settlers found him here when they came to hew their homes out of the bush. In those days he was a woodland bird. But I suppose it was soon discovered that he was an orchard bird, for he is very fond of fruit in season. Then, as towns grew into cities, the robin moved with the times and took to city dwelling. And here he is today, one of nature's own wild creatures living on friendly terms with us of the streets and sidewalks.

Those who have lived in England will be interested to learn that the robin of this land has been given his name because of the striking resemblance to the English robin. Both birds have red breasts so what was more natural than for a nature-loving pioneer, perhaps just a wee bit homesick, to look wistfully at this fine red-breasted thrush and call it a robin? And by now, who wants to change the name? Although he has had many changes in his scientific name, even to scientists he is the American Robin.

And now the sparrows. There were several near the robin, and what a difference! The genteel robin in his tasty colours and the drab commonplace little sparrows. I can think of no better analogy than a crowd of ragged little urchins capering about one of the guards of Whitehall in his splendid uniform and he, of course, remaining quite aloof amid their admiration.

But for all this somewhat odious comparison you may be surprised to learn that the sparrow has a much more impressive family history than the robin has. Insignificant and perhaps despised as he is today, he could, if he only knew it, point to a lineage which can be traced back to Biblical times. Is he not mentioned in several passages in Holy Writ? And there is every reason to believe that this is the very sparrow referred to. "Alone like a sparrow upon the housetop" would seem to indicate that even in those days this bird of the town sought the society of man.

And yet the sparrow is a comparative newcomer in this country. We call him the "English" sparrow, but he is really the house sparrow, for he is found not only in English towns but in all towns throughout Europe and parts of Asia. It seems that about 1850 a man from Brooklyn N.Y. had been travelling in the old country and was attracted by the sparrow—no one now knows why he should have been—and he conceived the unhappy idea of introducing this bird to America. The first attempts failed. Oh, that all subsequent attempts had also failed! But it happened that the city of Philadelphia at that time was grievously afflicted with a very destructive caterpillar known as the "span worm" which bid fair to strip the city's shade-trees of leaves. So the sparrow was hailed as a solution to the problem. It seems strange to us now to think of the superficial thought that was given to the matter. Any boy-naturalist today can tell you that the sparrow with that large conical beak is intended by nature to crack open and eat seeds. He is not an insectivorous bird. But nobody seems to have thought of that, so the English sparrow, as he was called, was imported wholesale and liberated to find his way in a new land.

He did. He has become the most successful nuisance ever introduced into this fair land. Far and away beyond the expectations of anyone concerned, this quick-witted, resourceful, aggressive little bird thrived and multiplied until now he seems to say, "Well I'm here now and you know why I'm here, and if you don't like me, what are you going to do about it?" And what can we do? We, who are his enemies, are his best friends. We feed him on our garbage. We leave him nooks and crannies about buildings that he may nest in safety. Living as he does so closely associated with man, he has ample protection from his natural enemies. Heat and cold and all sorts of weather seem the same to him, so he need not make the long hazardous journey southward annually. In short, like many another colonist in a new land, he has done well.

It is interesting to note that the sparrows I watched were hopping, not running, as was the robin, and that they were eating dandelion seeds. So we can at least give him credit for that. But I believe we would forgive him a great deal if he only had a voice, a good clear musical song of some kind instead of that incessant, harsh, unmusical chirp which we hear twelve months of the year.

Of course there were starlings to be seen, for they are everywhere nowadays. The starling is another immigrant that has done well in this new land. It seems hard to believe that only twenty years ago there were no starlings here in Ontario and forty years ago none in the United States. Apparently someone in New York thought it would be a fine thing to see European starlings in Central Park, so some hundred and twenty birds were imported and liberated. The experiment has been a disastrous success. The starlings increased so that they were soon seen not only in all New York City, but all New York State. About 1919 they reached Brockville, Ont. A year later they were reported at St. Catharines and Toronto. I recall myself seeing a flock of dark birds which I recognized as starlings, my first observation of their species in Ontario.

Since that time the birds have increased in such numbers that starlings are now believed to be the most abundant and most generally distributed species in all Ontario. We see them in towns and cities, about buildings and on lawns, As we drive along roads we find them settled and feeding in flocks in fields or sitting in rows along fences. As many people living in residential districts know, starlings have a habit of roosting in enormous numbers in shade trees and making the evening hideous by their chattering. As I sit in my garden in the evening I see dense flocks of the birds flying swiftly over the city from their feeding spots to roost about city buildings. Again, early in the morning, I see them returning in the same large flocks to feed. Everywhere and at all times starlings are in evidence, and all these from a hundred and twenty birds imported to one city in 1890.

It is not difficult to see the reason for such success in life, as it might be called, at least from the starling's point of view. He is a strong, vigorous, active, aggressive, greedy bird, apparently determined to succeed, and not particular by what means. His only real competitor in the city is no match for him. If a pair of starlings want to nest in a certain site, occupied by sparrows, the sparrows just have to get out. And here we touch on the chief menace of the starling. It is not his food habits, or his disagreeable congregating, or his spluttering unmusical notes, but the fact that he wants, and will have by force, the nesting sites of more desirable native species. The bluebird, the flicker, the crested flycatcher and the purple martin must make way for him, the undesirable interloper.

As I watched him on the lawn that evening, walking—not running as the robin, or hopping as the sparrow, but walking—about in his preoccupied manner, snatching a morsel here and there with no one but himself in mind and with no time for anything but his own affairs, I wonder why anybody thinking himself a bird-lover should have chosen this objectionable species over all the beautiful ones to adorn Central Park. And that after the experience with the house sparrow!

Now just a word about the lone flicker seen on that lawn. He was the oddest and most brilliantly clad of all, with his brown back barred in black, his buff breast spotted in black, yellow-quilled wing-feathers and scarlet nape-patch. And he himself was most out of place! The flicker is a woodpecker and should be in the woods, but having a mind of his own and being an original fellow, he often comes to the ground and that day he was, as I found out on investigation, digging out a nest of ants. In this his long, strong bill served him well, as he pecked into the ant-hills, but his short, long-clawed toes gave him a very awkward gait. This handsome woodpecker is a true native species. Early in April he comes to us from the south, announcing his arrival with a loud hilarious cackle. Then later he makes himself ridiculous with his curious courting manners as he tumbles about to display his various colours before some chosen lady flicker, uttering the queer swishing note of "Which chew, which chew."

So we had a motley group on the lawn—the thrush family represented by the genteel robin, the finches by the drab little sparrows, the starling representing his family, the starlings, and the woodpeckers represented by the lone flicker—all gathered there in the prosaic business of finding a living. After all, they were not unlike our own human communities. Are we not of many different families, creeds, colours and races, each with our own histories and backgrounds, gathered here to make a living?

Militant caterpillar

Walking twig

Nature's seed sowing

Ramble eleven

A FRIEND of mine was showing several of us through his garden on a lovely September day. Everything we saw was in the fresh maturity of early autumn. As we paused by a patch of parsley our friend pointed to a place where the leaves had been eaten away by a caterpillar, then, parting the leaves, he showed us the little marauder eating below.

It was a striking-looking creature about two inches long, pale green in colour, banded with black and yellow cross-lines. And yet, in its striped coat, it was difficult to see amid the criss-cross network of the parsley leaves.

"Why don't you kill it?" asked one of the party.

"I am going to let it spin its cocoon and have the fun of watching it come out as a butterfly," said our gardener-friend. "This caterpillar turns into a swallowtail, the beautiful black and yellow butterfly with tails on his wings."

After we had all admired the caterpillar the naturalist said: "Do you know the baleful secret of this despoiler of my parsley?" Then he teased the insect with his finger and, to our surprise, we saw two yellow horns shoot out from behind its head and at once a strong musty odour arose.

"Can you smell anything?" he asked.

"Smell anything?" exclaimed the one of the party farthest off. "I can smell it away over here."

"That," said our naturalist friend, "is the caterpillar's means of defence. He is so plump and smooth that he offers a tempting morsel to any of his enemies. But the moment he is molested he makes himself so thoroughly disagreeable by his offensive smell that they have long since learned to leave him alone."

"Just like the skunk?" suggested one.

"Yes," said the naturalist. "But the skunk is not the only animal in the woods with a fragrant personality. The mink, and the weasel too, can make themselves objectionable. It happens that the skunk is better known to most people."

"Nature has given animals many ways of protecting themselves from enemies," he continued. "The larger animals actually possess weapons, many of which are very effective. Think of the elephant with his tusks, the rhinoceros with his terrible horn, and the cat tribe—lions, tigers, leopard, and even puss sunning herself on the doorstep—all these have claws which they can extend at will when the occasion demands. The members of the dog family—wolves, foxes, coyotes—have not sharp claws, but they do their fighting with their teeth. Then the deer are provided with elaborate sets of horns which they can use in self-defence. The moose, the elk, and the red deer are good examples. These animals not only fight desperately with their antlers but can strike telling blows with their sharp hoofs."

"But," asked one of us, "does nature intend all animals to fight, as she provides them with weapons as you describe?"

"Oh, no," replied our informant. "Some animals are defensively armed. They don't attack, they simply ward off enemies. Our little friend, the caterpillar here, as one of you remarked, is like the skunk. Another creature that has a very effective means of defence is the porcupine; he never attacks, but with his formidable coat of quills, he can make himself a very awkward customer to deal with. The fox, the wolf, and the lynx all know better than to attack 'porky' in his armour of tiny bayonets."

"Can the porcupine shoot its quills at an enemy?" asked one of the party eagerly.

"No," came the scornful reply. "Not any more than you can shoot the hairs out of your head. That notion comes from the fact that, when molested, the porcupine will often slap its tail upwards, and this action leaves some quills sticking in whatever part of the enemy the tail happens to hit."

"Well, there's a point I've learned," said the questioner.

"This subject is really a very interesting part of natural history," continued our entertaining friend. "There are many different ways in which nature has endowed her creatures for their protection; weapons of offence, such as tusks, horns, hoofs, claws and teeth; and of defence such as quills, spines and odours. But did you ever hear of that means of protection which, though neither of these, does no harm to the enemy and yet is most effective of all?"

"And what is that?" we all asked.

"Oh, it's very simple. It consists of the animal being very much the same colour as its surroundings, and in keeping still when danger is near. Naturalists speak of it as 'protective coloration'.

By this means the brown cottontail rabbit in summer escapes his foes, and the white snowshoe rabbit is difficult to see in the winter woods. The partridge in its variegated plumage of browns and greys is rendered almost invisible to the hunter. There are many, many examples of this protective coloration as a means of safeguarding the weaker creatures."

"May I ask a question?" said one. "What means of protection has nature provided for the creature called man?"

"Well, the Good Book tells us 'Man was made upright, but he sought out many inventions'," said the naturalist seriously. "I suppose we might say that he was provided with two good fists to defend himself. Nature thought that would be enough. But it seems that man considers his own life so precious that there is no end of weapons which he has invented to kill his enemies at close quarters. And as for foes beyond his reach, he has constructed machine-guns, long-range guns, bombs, shells and mines, and even poison gas. It does seem incredible that with all our humane effort in other activities, with our intelligence and reason far beyond other creatures in nature, and all the teachings of our religion of love, we should deliberately plan to kill and maim our fellow men in ways unknown to nature in even her sternest mood."

I had a fine example of protective coloration on the day I received a parcel from someone living in the country which, when opened, revealed the strangest-looking creature one could imagine. It had a slim body about thee inches long. From its small head stood out two long feelers or antennae, and it walked upon six long spindly legs, which raised it about an inch above the table on which we placed it. It was difficult to think of the creature as really alive. When it stood still it appeared to be a mere lifeless stick with several smaller sticks attached to it, and all wood-brown in colour. I recognized it at once as the "Stick insect" or "Walking-stick" insect. As I watched it I could scarcely imagine a more appropriate name. The insect was a mere stick with branches that could walk. Strange to say this queer insect is related to the grasshopper, the cricket and the katydid, those nimble-footed, light-winged creatures known to us all, that flit and hop about the fields in the summer sunshine, trilling their little ditties. But how different is this stick insect! He pokes along on his long thin legs as awkwardly as a boy on stilts. And as for wings to bear him through the air—he just hasn't any. My naturalist friend explained to me that there was a time in the insect's history when he did have wings, but he has long since lost them, and now must tumble along on his pins and see his more fortunate relatives go sailing by on airy pinions.

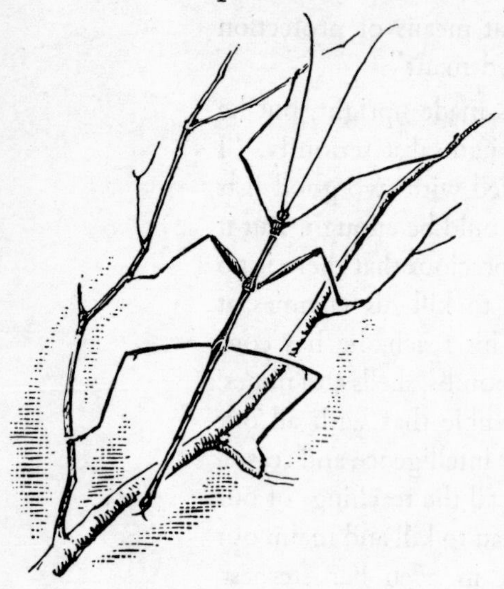

Late in summer, stick insects become very common. All the tiny pale-green baby insects, nymphs as they are called, have grown up and are scrambling about the bushes nibbling at the leaves. I suppose most of us have listened to the cheery notes of the crickets and the katydids chirping and trilling as they bask in the September sunshine. But we listen in vain for the song of the stick insect. He has neither voice nor instrument to play. It is as though at some time in his history he was the sulky music pupil who wouldn't practice, so the great teacher, Nature, took these gifts away from him. And now he is the most unmusical member of the whole family.

During the month of September the female drops her eggs. That is a queer thing to say about eggs, but it is exactly what she does. She simply drops them to the ground from wherever she happens to be, and leaves them to their fate. Most creatures take good care of their eggs and young by building nests or concealing their offspring. But mother stick insect cares as little about home duties as her husband does about music. So the eggs hatch out the next spring amid the fallen leaves of the previous autumn and the baby insects start life without ever seeing their mothers.

So the queer-looking stick insect, slow in movement and in wit, harmless and defenceless, has been made to look strangely like a twig, so that amid a maze of twigs he will be overlooked by his hungry enemies. You may say that you have never seen such an insect in all your life. Perhaps you have seen many and thought you were looking at twigs.

Did you ever think as you plucked a few burs from your clothing while out on a stroll and tossed them carelessly aside that you were doing just what nature intended you to do? Somewhere on your ramble you brushed against a bur-bush, collected a few burs, and now you have sowed them in a new spot. How ingenious of nature to adopt such a method! Look at the bur. It is a little globe thickly set with a multitude of tiny hooks arranged for clinging. But not to human garments only. Long before people were rambling, nature had learned that animals have long fur to which burs will cling, and these animals have learned to bite burs out of their coats only to sow them elsewhere just as we do.

There are many kinds and shapes of burs which will cling—the globular burdock with its tiny hooks, the oval clotbur with its rough spines, beggars' tick with its two long barbed prongs, and the rough little hound's tongue nutlet. Hook, spines, barbs and prongs all exist for the same purpose—clinging in order to be carried away and dropped to grow elsewhere.

In some cases the whole plant is borne off. Down in the low tangled shady woods grows the frail white-flowered galium or cleavers. Too weak to stand alone, it trails its way through the grass and low bushes. Though delicate-looking it is coarse and rough to the touch, being armed with thousands of microscopic barbs on its stem and branches. Should a cow or deer push through its haunts, the plant fastens itself upon the animal's coat and is instantly torn from its roots. Yards of the plant may thus be carried away to drop seeds to germinate elsewhere. No wonder it is named cleavers when it will be uprooted rather than release its hold.

Though the bur method is very successful for scattering seeds, we find nature has other methods. She knows that summer breezes can also be utilized. There seems to be no nook or cranny in all outdoors where, with the help of the zephyr, she cannot sow her seeds. So the sails are set and the seeds float away. The thistle, the dandelion, the milkweed, the aster and the goldenrod are all familiar examples. All these flowers bloom, fade, then spread their downy heads and await the breeze to bear their seeds off.

Not unlike these is the sombre cattail rush of the marsh which, though not flowering in quite the same way as other plants, raises its brown head amid the green herbage of the marsh and ripens its seeds all through the summer. Then in autumn thousands upon thousands of microscopic seeds lie close, each with its own silky sails tightly folded away. Day after day the pressure grows until the time comes when they must give way, and when they do the whole mass comes rolling out from the cylindrical head and the air all about becomes filled with silken-winged seeds that go floating down the breeze.

Birds and animals do their part in seed distribution. But nature does not ask them to work for nothing. She knows well that she must tempt them to help her. What a luscious morsel a ripe strawberry or raspberry is! Some day a robin or a waxwing will snatch it and bear it away to eat elsewhere. As the bird breaks up the fruit with its bill to eat it piecemeal, some seed-laden fragments will be sure to drop to earth to germinate next year.

Most of us have watched the active little red squirrel as he scrambles along a limb to seize an acorn or beechnut. Perhaps he is not hungry at the time, but very busy getting in the harvest. Trip after trip up and down the tree he makes, bearing nuts away from the branches to bury in the soil below. Surely he never can remember exactly where each nut is buried! And, as he does not mark the spots, there must be many nuts left in the ground to germinate into future trees. I remember once watching a red squirrel in the northern forest. Evergreen tree cones were his choice on this occasion. As I watched cone after cone go into the ground under his nimble paws, I saw in this active little rascal, whose reputation is none too good in other ways, the best co-operator we have in the worthy scheme of reforestation. Toiling away hour after hour in places and over areas man could never hope to cover, surely the red squirrels plant many miles of forests. Then I wondered if my little friend himself were not, even as I watched him, scrambling up and down the very spruce and balsam trees planted by his forefathers years ago.

Nature is as ingenious as she is resourceful. In her methods of scattering seeds some are unique, being used on one plant only. There is the common vetch or tare, a member of the pea family. The pretty little bunch of purple flowers fades away in a few days, giving place to black pods, each laden with peas. As they dry and become crisp in the summer sun, each pod is trying hard to spread its halves in opposite directions. The strain grows until suddenly they give way, and like a flash become as two spiral shavings. A moment sooner we would have found a row of ripe peas inside, but now they are scattered far and wide, like fragments of a bursting shell, which of course they really are.

Then there is the orange jewel-weed, a smooth, graceful plant of the bogs. Its showy orange flowers dangle gaily from their stalks. But what are those pale-green pods which hang here and there among the flowers? Touch one and see. If the pods are really ripe you may get a shock. What appeared to be a pod a moment ago in your fingers is now what seems to be several green curly worms. What happened? The curly "worms" are what used to be the sides of the pod. As the seeds inside were ripening the pod sides were drawing up tighter and tighter. But the central partition resisted all pressure—as long as it could. Then your touch shook the plant and the pod collapsed elastically with a snap, sending its seeds broadcast. Is the plant not well named "touch-me-not"?

But of all the strange ways in which plants shoot their seeds abroad none is so startling as that employed by the witch hazel. It would seem as though this original shrub actually contrived to be different from other plants in many of its habits. When most plants are bearing their harvests of seeds after flowering all summer, the witch hazel is blossoming out in all its glory. It is a common sight to see this bush a mass of golden glow in the October sun. Perhaps even its wilted leaves are shed, yet the flowers are blooming. A strange plant this, that spreads its blossoms to the same sun as it is ripening its seeds. We wonder how this can be.

A glance at the twigs tells us the story. Here is the flower, certainly not showy, for it consists of a mere woody rim with four yellow strips of petals forming a lank cross. Beside this odd flower we find on the same twig a couple of queer greenish knobs. These knobs were the flowers of last October. They bloomed, faded and spent all the following summer ripening into these knobs or witch-hazel nuts (not to be confused with hazel nuts). As the days go by, these nuts split across one end and disclose two shiny black seeds. Wider and wider the split becomes, opening into a sort of grotesque grin. As the grin widens the nut presses in on its sides against the two seeds. With this growing pressure something must give way. Then, with a sharp "click" which can be plainly heard, the seeds are shot through the air ten, fifteen, or even twenty feet, just as a schoolboy will pinch a slippery orange seed and send it flying across the schoolroom. Surely it is not by chance that this unique bush which blooms in an off-season, with such queer flowers, and scatters its seeds in such an ingenious way from grotesquely grinning pods, is named "witch" hazel!

These are but a few of the various methods which nature employs to spread her seeds abroad. And when we consider the infinite variety of plants finding root and flourishing in every available spot, we must admit that her methods are not wanting in efficiency.

September joys

Northern shrike

Cocoon hunting

The charms of sound

Ramble twelve

EACH month of the year has its own quota of life, and in mellow September we see nature as she is at no other time. Perhaps the one thing we miss most in the bird world is the songs of the birds. There are still plenty of birds to be seen. In fact there are really more birds than in spring, for in addition to their parents, there are all the young of the year flying about. But the song season is passed. These September days are silent. We do not hear the full chorus of springtime. Somehow as long as flowers bloom and trees are in green leaf we feel that the birds should still be singing. Even in August, though it is largely a songless month, we still hear the last few notes of the red-eyed vireo and the wood pewee. The whippoorwill may chant in a feeble way. But these are the closing notes of the season. September comes to us as the bright, yet songless, month.

The fall migration is getting under way. Many of our birds are gathering in flocks, preparing for their journey southward. The blackbird family is a great one to flock. Perhaps you have noticed bands of bobolinks flying overhead in September. They are small birds of a buff colour and as they pass over we hear their simple call of "Tink, tink," which now replaces the bubbling burst of song we associate with this bird of the meadows. Down in the reedy marshes where the cattails are now standing so high and dense we find great flocks of cowbirds, starlings and redwings. All day they have been travelling about the country and now find these marshes with their dense growth of reeds ample shelter for the chilly September evenings. The various swallows also gather here, and as they fly round and round before settling down for the night they seem as abundant as gnats.

One of the most interesting sights in the bird world during September is the spectacular migration of the hawks. The bright cool days of this month seem to tempt these birds to be on their way. We see the larger species, the red-shouldered, the red-tailed and the broad-winged hawks, flying high overhead. It is really an inspiring sight to watch these big birds passing westward over the country. Around and around they fly in wide graceful circles, perfect pictures of repose in motion. The smaller hawks, among which are the sharp-shinned, the Cooper's and the pigeon hawk, do not soar and circle high in the air, but skim along lower and closer to the ground.

There are many birds from all over the country migrating in September, but no bird movement is so conspicuous, so easily watched and, to the bird-lover, so fascinating as the hawk migration. I regret to say, however, that no class of our birds has been so misjudged and, as a consequence of unreasoning prejudice and persecution, these splendid birds have been much reduced in numbers. We do not often see the great flights today that were seen in former times.

But though September may be a songless month it is not quite silent. Most birds utter call-notes at any time and during migration these call-notes serve to keep the birds together. Some species actually give us short fragments of song. With these I believe this is irrepressible. For example, almost any summer day we can hear the purple finch singing his loud, free, flowing warble. With such a vigorous songster it is not surprising, then, that we hear a few odd bars of his song even as late in the fall as dull November. I remember one gloomy fall day scrambling eagerly up a steep hillside in the woods to learn what bird was singing, only to find a small flock of purple finches feeding on some wild fruit. There was one fine male among them warbling the odd notes I had heard.

A year or so ago I was out on a Labour Day holiday and came upon a flock of chickadees. They were active and enjoying life as chickadees usually do. As they travelled along through the woods they twittered cheerily in the call-notes I have spoken of. Now whenever I meet chickadees I always speak to them; so I whistled a bar or two of their spring song. At once they were interested and seemed puzzled. Here was their spring song being sung in September. Surely there must be some misunderstanding. Then one irrepressible chickadee answered, not in the clear sweet tones of spring, but somewhat huskily and sounding a little out-of-date.

Occasionally we hear the white-throat sing in the fall. Everyone knows the sweet plaintiff note of this beautiful sparrow, singing in the spring. In September we find the white-throat journeying along the hedgerows with other sparrows on migration. Should you whistle even the poorest imitation of his song you will very likely get an answer in a few faltering bars that recall to mind, though faintly, the full musical melody of May and June. So if you are planning to learn bird music, do not begin during your summer holidays, for you may have a discouraging time of it at your music lessons. For in the heat of midsummer as in September it is only the bolder songsters who break the general silence of the hushed air.

Yet September *is* a musical month. The air is filled with music other than bird notes, music we do not hear amid the midsummer heat and which will be hushed in chilly October. A music which comes from myriads of humbler musicians little known to any except the nature-lover. The next time you are out for a walk in the fields or some overgrown vacant lot, or even your own garden during the bright September days, pause and listen. If your ears are attuned to detect minute sounds you will hear all about you the ringing symphony of tiny notes. So tiny are they that their combined effect has been spoken of as "audible silence." Every year as the sunny days of this splendid month come around this symphony begins. It is so much a part of September's atmosphere that we are inclined to accept it as a matter of course, that is if we hear it at all!

Who are these humble musicians? Many kinds of insects, each contributing the notes of his own musical instrument to the chorus. Some of these notes are fairly loud and can be heard some distance away. Others are lower but with enough volume to be easily heard. But many are high-pitched and thin. And some are so still and small as to be almost inaudible. The music may be sung as a continuous trill or in vibrating bars or chirps. But when all blend together the air resounds with the music of these lowly musicians.

Best-known of these and certainly the loudest is the note of the cicada, which was discussed in an earlier chapter. His song is heard during the heat of midsummer and continues into the warm days of September.

There are several kinds of large green grasshoppers often called "katydids" which give us good music in September. Each species has notes of his own. And when we consider that all perform in the same manner, by chafing their rough wings together, it is remarkable that some many different types of music can be produced. Yet a practised ear can readily distinguish these and tell which species is "singing".

The well-known black cricket is also one of September's musicians. In fact, so closely is this little insect associated with its music that the word "cricket" is derived from a Dutch word meaning "chirp". In the Old Country, crickets often find their way into houses and have made themselves very much at home near warm ovens and fireplaces where their chirping has become an accepted sound in the household. Some of you may have had this little guest-musician in your home, whom you have often heard but never seen.

And then there are the tree crickets, delicate green creatures with light gauze-like wings. These pretty little creatures give us the most pleasing of all insect music. They are found on trees and bushes—that is, if they are found at all. Their light-green colour makes them very difficult to see, and they are so shy that the moment they think that they are being watched their music ceases. You may know full well that you are within a few inches of the singing insect, and can hear his mellow song clearly, yet you can see nothing of him. Still the music goes on, then all at once it ceases and there is silence. The timid little musician has seen you and has hastily put his violin away. There will be no more music until he feels he is alone again.

Among the many flowers which bloom in September there are two which we cannot fail to notice, the goldenrods and the asters. Both come into their glorious perfection in the mellow days of late summer. Everyone knows the goldenrod with its handsome yellow flowers growing so profusely that whole fields become golden with their bloom. There are many varieties of this plant, all with golden flowers except one, whose flowers are creamy white. This plant is called "silverrod", thus distinguishing it from the other in the family.

The asters are even more beautiful than the goldenrods. They grow in many different situations. In the open fields, by the shrubby fence corners, in the woods, on the hillsides, and some in swampy places. And what is more fortunate for those of us who would learn their names, these flowers differ widely in their colours. There is the sky-blue swamp aster; a long-stemmed variety that is lavender in colour, growing on wet, grassy shores; the heart-leaved and the arrow-leaved asters, both with delicate purple flowers; a few pink ones, and many that are plain white; and the most beautiful of all, the New England aster, with its many flowers of rich violet-purple. And, strange to say, there is one that seems like a connecting link between the asters and the goldenrods—the golden aster, with its flowers of bright yellow.

Do you remember my telling you of how I came upon a mouse caught upon a thorn? Perhaps you wondered how such a humble little creature, which generally keeps out of sight, should get himself into such dire straits. Let me assure you it was not the mouse's choice. This is how the tragedy happened.

Late in the autumn many birds come down from the north. Some pass on to their winter homes in the far south. Others pause here and spend the winter with us. Among these many migrants there is a long-tailed, greyish bird with a black mask. Although he is among them, he is not one of them. The many kinds of sparrows, those gleaners of the stubble fields and weed-patches, keep a sharp look-out for this black-masked brigand, for they never know the moment when he will appear and, swooping down, snatch one of them in his hooked bill and bear his victim off.

After a few weeks the sparrow flocks move on to the south. But the brigand does not follow them. He simply changes his menu. The brown fields turn to white with the first fall of snow. This helps him in his hunting. Day after day we see him on some favourite observation-post overlooking the broad scene before him. He is keenly alert, watching every little brown tuft of grass which shows above the snow. And what remarkable sight the bird must have! The moment a mouse appears, ten, twenty, even fifty yards away, this keen-eyed monster is after him. Perhaps the mouse is rash enough to make a dash for the next grass-tuft. He may never get there. The track on the snow tells the tale of a struggle and shows a drop of blood. He was caught and borne away to the nearest thorn bush, to be impaled there.

Who is this feathered murderer, and why this strange habit of thus hanging up his victims? His proper name is the shrike, the northern shrike, but he is also well named the "butcher-bird." As a bird of prey he seems to be but half equipped by nature. He has a hooked hawk-like bill, but the feet of a perching bird. With such a bill he can easily seize and carry off his prey, but he must find some way to hold it securely while he devours it piecemeal. To this end he has learned to make use of the sharp thorns growing on the many bushes near his hunting ground. A true hawk would hold his victim firmly in his strong claws, needing no thorns.

But it may be that the shrike is not very hungry at the time of catching the mouse, so he leaves it hanging like the one I found. But what is to prevent some other shrike finding the mouse and dining first? Perhaps this does happen sometimes. But then again, there may be such a thing as honour among shrikes, as there is said to be among thieves.

So, now you know the story about the mouse upon the thorn—the tragedy in one act.

And how, you ask, did the shrike, denied by nature the strong sharp claws of a true bird of prey, learn to make use of thorns in place of claws? We may never learn this. Necessity seems to be the mother of invention even in nature's outdoor kingdom. However he learned it, we believe this is one of the few cases in which a wild bird has learned to use a tool.

The melancholy days are come, the saddest of the year,
Of wailing winds and naked woods and meadows brown and sear.

So sang the poet Bryant of the autumn season. In his mind he was comparing sombre autumn with joyous spring and summer. But Bryant was more a poet than a naturalist. For the naturalist there are no "melancholy days." He has learned that each season, yes, each month outdoors, however it may be to most people, has its unique charm and interest.

It is quite true that during the melancholy days of which Bryant speaks we cannot ramble afield and enjoy the bright flowers of spring, the fruits of summer, or the glorious tints of autumn. But in dull leafless November and December there are still interesting things to find which prove to be real treasures.

Some sombre autumn day you may be out on a ramble and notice a strange object clinging to the twigs. It is a cocoon, and though apparently lifeless, it is quite alive and for you holds a delightful secret to be learned later.

Cocoons are the winter homes of those insects we call moths. All through the leafy days of summer the caterpillar ate and ate until he felt the time had come when he must seal himself up for the winter. So, choosing a suitable spot, he wove around himself a tight silken garment. You and I would not choose silk for winter wear, but so closely does he weave that his garment is not only very tough but also insulates him from the severest frosts. The one danger that he does face is that some bright-eyed downy woodpecker may find his retreat and drive his sharp bill into it in search of food. To guard against this calamity many caterpillars wrap their cocoons about with the nearby leaves, which remain clinging to the cocoon after they are dead, thus concealing it. And this gives you a clue in your search! Do not look for the cocoon but for the bundle of leaves and you will find the cocoon within.

There are many shapes and sizes of cocoons, just as there are many sizes and colours of moths. Some are fastened to bare twigs, some hidden amid leaves as described, others dangle from silken cords, and several species of caterpillars spin their cocoons in

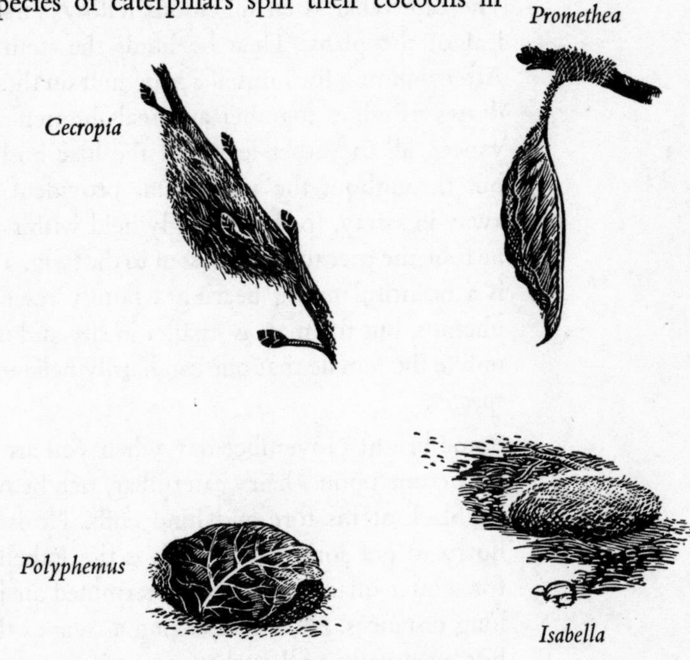

holes in the ground or under a log or stone. So the searching out of these trophies becomes a fascinating treasure-hunt and their finding worthy of sharp eyes.

The largest of our cocoons is the Cecropia's. It is about four inches long, dull brown and spindle-shaped. It is firmly attached to the twig, often in plain view. The Cecropia is one of our largest moths, measuring over five inches across its extended wings. Its colours are grey and brown with a striking bar of pink and white across both pairs of wings which are also conspicuously spotted with the same colours. Though not rare, its large size and unique markings create interest whenever the insect is found.

Another large cocoon you may find is that of the Polyphemus. This moth is a beautiful insect. Its wings are a soft brown tint with pale brown borders. On each wing there is a clear transparent spot like a tiny window. Though not as large as the Cecropia, it is, I think, the more beautiful of the two. This cocoon is elliptical in shape, firmly attached to a twig and generally concealed in several leaves.

The winter quarters of the Promethea moth is a curiously constructed affair. It is often found on the bush of the common lilac. The caterpillar is an ingenious fellow. First he chooses a single leaf of the plant. Then he binds the stem firmly to the twig. After spinning for himself a snug nest on the surface of the leaf, he draws its edges together and seals himself in. As the season advances, all the other leaves of the lilac bush wilt and fall away, but throughout the winter this provident little spinner swings away in safety, for he is snugly held within his leaf-cradle which he took the precaution to fasten to the twig. The female Promethea is a beautiful moth, bearing a family resemblance to the Polyphemus, but the male is smaller in size and is dull dark brown, so unlike the female that one can hardly believe them to be the same species.

Some bright November day when you are out for a walk, you may come upon a hairy caterpillar, rich brown in the middle and jet black at his fore and hind ends. He is generally in a great hurry to get some place. This is the Isabella caterpillar looking for winter quarters. With a determined air he crawls and crawls long distances. He is not seeking a twig as the others mentioned, but eventually will curl up in some cosy nook under a log or stone and there will spin a rough cocoon of his own hair. Next spring he will emerge a fine rich orange-yellow moth, with delicate veining on his wings.

These are but a few of the cocoons you may find while on a ramble during Bryant's "melancholy days." There are many others, and finding them is good fun and splendid training for your powers of observation. Besides, there is nothing like having an object on any ramble.

But finding the cocoons is only half your reward. Some time later in the winter or early spring you may hear a strange scratching within one of your winter-gathered cocoons. Watch closely, for a miracle is about to happen before your very eyes.

Out from an opening now being made in the end of the cocoon there crawls, not the energetic caterpillar who worked so hard to seal himself in, but the weirdest-looking creature imaginable. It is clothed with coloured down, has six legs instead of many, and two pairs of bedraggled wings which hang limply from its back. Can this be the moth? How different from the light airy creatures we know which flutter and sail through the evening air! Where are the magnificent wings? Wait. Mother Nature bids this unkempt creature bestir itself, for these are precious moments in its life, moments it must not neglect if it is to become the perfect insect she intends it should. Soon the newly emerged moth commences to wave its wings gently, and though they are small at first we can almost see them grow. They lose their limpness and become larger and larger until, wonder of wonders, before our very eyes, the sorry bedraggled creature of a few moments ago has been transformed into a beautiful full-grown moth with splendid wings which bear it aloft into that airy world above that the lowly caterpillar never knew.

Every nature-lover knows the secret of the "medicine bag." That bundle of balsam, that spray of cedar, the field of new-mown hay, how their odours bring memories of other days surging through our beings! Again we feel the lure of the northern forest, the charm of the pastural landscape. Science tells us that, of all our senses, the sense of smell is most closely connected with the faculty of memory.

But the sense of hearing can claim a place here, too. For does not the ringing of the old school bell bring to mind vividly days of long ago? Perhaps this was in Tennyson's mind when he wrote those wistful lines:

> *But oh for the touch of a vanished hand,*
> *And the sound of a voice that is still!*

Sometimes I think sounds call into being as we listen, another faculty, that of imagination. The sense of smell may recall actual scenes and experiences long since vanished. In the same way sounds do so too. But further, they bring up scenes and impressions which exist largely in imagination. Should the sound we hear fit some scene we know, well and good. But it may fit no such scene, so imagination conjures up one to fit the sound.

This came to me vividly as I was strolling about the hillsides of the river near my home. It was a bright November day. In my ramble I happened to pause for a few moments where there stood two trees, a white oak and a white pine. The leaves of the oak were still clinging to the tree, brown and sere, rustling in the breeze. I stopped under the tree to listen to their music. In it I heard a sound which spoke of a bright autumn day, cool and invigorating, with its acres of brown fields and hillsides and sombre woods before me, all soon to feel the touch of frost and death. They rustled merrily, those leaves. Though they must soon fall, there was an indescribable charm in their rustling. How well the sound fitted into the scene before me now! It was part of it.

Then I stepped under the pine, with its green needles that know not death in autumn. There was no rustle here, but a soft, sighing whistle as the needles cut the breeze. As I listened I did not see the bright, cool days of autumn in this land, but the dark, bleak days of winter and death in some foreign clime. For some unaccountable reason—perhaps because of childhood stories—visions of Russia rose before me, with cold and snow and darkness everywhere. This sighing sound of the pine needles fitted into weird tales of dark stretches of gloomy woods and endless plains of snow with the doleful howling of wolves—all that we shrink from.

How different was the effect of two sounds essentially the same—the wind blowing through the leaves of two different trees!

Downy woodpecker
Partridge in winter
Muskrat

At first glance we might think that the woodpeckers have dull, uninteresting lives. Nature seems to have condemned them to the awkward attitude of clinging upright to the limbs and trunks of trees instead of perching gracefully on a limb. And while other birds are picking their insect food daintily from the leaves and twigs or adroitly snatching a flying insect, the hard-working woodpecker, it appears, is forced to chisel his fare out of the wood itself.

But nature knows what she is doing. She has given the woodpecker family a department all to themselves. The little black-and-white downy woodpecker is the one of his family which we most often see in the orchard and shade trees. As we watch him, we learn much about the life of all his relatives. We soon see that it is their business to "nip mischief in the bud." That is to destroy the insect pests in their early stages. So, the hard-working downy gets food by hard pecking.

However, this chisel-like bill serves him well in other ways. He has learned that with the same bill he can excavate for himself a

large comfortable place in the wood of a dead tree and there rear his family in safety from both storms and enemies. And when winter comes and insects are no longer to be found outdoors, the downy remains with us throughout the bleak season and still finds plenty of food by his pecking and fashions for himself a cosy retreat from cold and storm within the tree-trunk.

In other ways, too, he has proved himself to be a resourceful little bird. Somehow he has discovered that grubs are to be found in places other than tree-trunks. There are certain insects which deposit their eggs in the tender pith of flower-stalks. The common yellow goldenrod is one of the plants often selected. At the proper time the parent insect stings the growing plant and deposits an egg deep in the pith. The plant thus irritated grows a large knob on the affected part. In nature study this is called a "gall." This gall is really the home of the tiny grub which is eating away within. He may appear to be quite safe in there, eating and growing, but the bright-eyed downy woodpecker knows the meaning of those galls on the stems of the goldenrod.

One day he finds a patch of those stems having galls. At once he sets to work; "Tap, tap, tap," goes his chisel-bill. Goldenrod stalks, dry and dead in winter, are easy material for a bill used for hard wood. One after another the retreats are attacked, and the little white hermits within are dug out and eaten. Had they been left to mature, they would have developed to be winged insects and perhaps would have been seized in flight by some flycatcher family the next summer.

Such is the downy's work, this winter foraging, and the fat little grub eating away within the goldenrod gall is only one item on his bill-of-fare. To us this little incident is a bit of bird-study, of insect-study and of botany all in one.

Most of us find a great deal of pleasure in watching the wild folk of the woods during the day. Birds flit here and there calling and singing. Squirrels scamper about chattering at us. Everywhere there is abundant life. But did you ever think where all these bright active creatures spend the night? When Mother Nature draws her curtain and darkness settles over all, where do they all go? In nooks and crannies and all sorts of odd places each finds for itself a safe retreat until another day breaks.

Many of our smaller birds find abundant shelter in the evergreens. These friendly trees with their thick foliage provide security at all seasons of the year. The woodpecker, as he know, has long since learned to hew out a cavity in some tree-trunk where he may return as evening comes on. I can imagine occasions when the bird finds a red squirrel already curled up for the night. What an altercation must follow! But then "possession is nine points of the law."

Few birds solve the problem of a night's lodging more easily than the ruffed grouse or partridge. All year round his home is in the woods. At night in spring, summer and autumn he simply flies up and roosts in the lower branches, secure from the foxes, weasels and minks prowling below and hidden from owls by the network of leaves and twigs above. But what of the leafless winter? This season of death does not trouble the partridge at all. At its approach nature provides him with a pair of dainty snow-shoes in the form of a comb-like fringe along both sides of each of his long toes. He is now able to walk on the top of the snow instead of sinking into it, and high enough to reach the nourishing buds which were far above his head formerly. Then at evening, when the blue shadows lengthen across the snow, the partridge chooses a smooth clear space in the woods and actually dives into the snow-drift for the night. The same snow which raised him to his food during the day, now becomes his warm protecting blanket at night.

One winter afternoon I was out for a snowshoe tramp in Manitoba. We were making our way through what is called in that country a "bluff," that is, a clump of trees. It was just about sunset. As we tramped along we were startled by a loud "whirr-r-r." Off through the woods we saw a brown form flying away. It was a partridge, that we knew, but where had he come from? We should have seen his brown form on the snow. But the bird had not been *on* the snow but *in* it. Then we found the snowy impression that revealed the whole story. He had not walked into his bed, nor had he nestled down for fear of leaving tell-tale marks. He actually dived in head first, and there out of sight he had snuggled down in his snowy coverlet. But soon he heard footsteps approaching and sprang "out of bed," clear through the snow into the air, leaving only the wing-marks on the surface as he skimmed away to safety.

Of course in sleeping out—if you can call it "out"—like this, there are certain risks. A prowling fox may happen along and should the partridge be too sound asleep to hear the soft patter of furry paws—very much quieter than the crunch of snowshoes—the hunter may discover the open hole in the snow. But even so, how is he to know just where the partridge lies beneath, or at what point the bird will whirr forth?

Another danger is the possibility of a cold rain falling during the night, sealing over the snow with a firm coating of ice, thus preventing the partridge from coming out in the morning. Sometimes this happens with fatal results to many little sleepers in the snow.

But why, you wonder, does not the partridge seek out some thick clump of evergreens and there sleep free from all the dangers of the ground? Undoubtedly he does, where evergreens grow, but in the Manitoba bluffs grow poplar, ash and birch only, which shed their leaves and have naked branches all winter. So the wise partridge seeks a bed where he will be snug and safe and certainly hidden.

One Christmas Day some years ago I went for a ramble through the river valley near my home. My object was to see how many birds were to be found on this winter morning, for Christmas was the day on which many of us all over the country took our bird "census." The weather was certainly not inviting. A raw east wind was blowing and with it fell a light wet snow. No glimpse of the sun cheered the bleak landscape or warmed the chill air. One might easily say, "What a day to go on a pleasure hike, surely nothing will be astir in such weather as this!" Yet the first thing I saw as I came to the river's edge was, not a bird, but something I expected much less to see. There, half in and half out of the icy water of the river with its frozen edges of shore-line, sat a fine muskrat.

He was nibbling away on a bit of root, evidently enjoying this cheerless repast as much as I expected to enjoy my cheery Christmas dinner later in the day. I crept close to the bank and watched

him as he ate. When he had finished the root he deliberately struck out across the river to the opposite side, and, plunging beneath the surface, he disappeared into a hole in the bank. As I walked away I could not help thinking what a drab existence nature has allotted the muskrat, that he must spend his time, night and day, winter and summer, amid watery surroundings.

But I have long since learned to believe that every creature enjoys life just as well as any of its neighbours. The pond, the marsh, the river, wherever it may be that he has chosen for his home—the muskrat knows no better place. Most likely he was born there, so he clings to its friendly bosom, knowing well that sheet of water is his best friend On its broad surface he can travel wherever he likes. Its reeds and rootlets, growing all about, form his bill of fare. Should an enemy appear he escapes by merely plunging beneath its surface. If the enemy presses him, he seeks safety in a hole in the bank and vanishes amid a cloud of muddy water. But, you think, he must always be as wet as a "drowned rat." No, with all this water-travelling he is always dry, for he has two coats; his top coat is of hard shiny brown hair, and below this is another of thick grey wool. No doubt the outer coat gets wet as our overcoats do, but the woollen undergarment he wears allows no water to penetrate. So that on this Christmas morning my muskrat was not only quite dry but cosy and warm even amid such bleak surroundings.

Generally speaking the muskrat is a quiet peaceable animal. With several neighbours he lives in his watery home, minding his own business and never seeming to have any misunderstandings with other creatures. He would rather dive than fight. Well he knows that this pond-home with its forest of reeds above and below—like the ancient cities of refuge—has open arms to receive him in times of danger when hard pressed by foes. And what foes he has! Above fly the sharp-eyed, sharp-clawed hawks by day; and by night those keen-eyed ogres, the owls. These are easily dealt with. Their power to harm ends at the surface. Below he is safe. The same can be said of foxes, wolves and dogs, even of the man with the gun. But that savage hunter, the dreaded otter, is as much at home in the water as on land. Swimming and diving the muskrat can escape him only by getting into the nearest bank-hole, where the larger animal cannot enter. The mink is an enemy indeed. He has all the aquatic powers of the muskrat and is able, with his long slim body, to pursue his victim far into the winding depths of the tunnel. I can hardly imagine a more terrible encounter than that which takes place between a hungry mink and a desperate muskrat in a death struggle in such narrow quarters, which may or may not be under water.

If it were not for enemies—and all creatures have them in numbers—the muskrat would live a blissful, contented life. Several of them finding themselves in the same marsh do not dispute its ownership. They accept each other's company on equal terms and not only live peaceably but combine forces to carry on community work. Highways are built, that is, ways are forced through the growth of aquatic reeds. These are like steamboat channels. Some lead to open water, some to feeding spots, and perhaps several to the home-lodge in the centre of the pond. The next time you stand on some bank overlooking a likely marsh, look for the muskrat's swimming-paths on the weedy surface, and try to trace out their systems and where they lead. Be sure to look for the little haycock-like house of piled weeds, which is storehouse, nursery and rest-room all in one.

Not only do they live together but muskrats plan to meet each other. With almost the intelligence of community spirit they toil away building landing places or docks. These are little muddy spots where the animals can readily come ashore and, what is more important, get off shore quickly in case of enemies. I have no doubt that each voyager on landing noses about, and by means of his keen sense of smell, can tell who has been there lately. So the little dock becomes a news centre.

All of us are familiar with the awful stench made by the skunk when disturbed, and perhaps many of us know that the mink and the weasel can make themselves intolerable on occasion. We have therefore learned to associate animals which wear fur with powerful and disagreeable odours. But true to his quiet sociable nature, the muskrat imparts good will to his kind, a message laden with the sweet incense of friendship, the perfume of musk. Other furbearers may have a bad reputations, but the muskrat has won for himself the name of *musk* rat solely through his fragrant personality.

As long as there is plenty of water in the muskrat colony all is well. But whereas most of us fear a flood, the muskrat fears a drought. During a long dry summer I can imagine the swimmers anxiously watching the edges of their pond creeping in and in, day after day, until the limpid home becomes no more than shiny mud, the friendly holes in the banks high and dry and there is no more swimming. Then there are hard times in the muskrat world. One after another the members leave and, much against their will, travel overland seeking a new home.

It is now the muskrat becomes an enemy of all. He seems to know that he is at a hopeless disadvantage without the friendly water. Swimming, diving and hiding no longer possible, he becomes a desperate and dangerous fighter. Even horses in a pas-

ture field have been attacked by a wandering muskrat in search of a new home. There is a story told of a boy who was set upon by a muskrat while walking along a road. The animal ran at him, biting one foot then the other, as fast as it was shaken off. Finally it was killed by an umbrella the boy was carrying. It must have been a terrible battle, for the writer of the story remarks that he saw both the rat and the umbrella after and "there was not much left of either." However, this ferocious fighting seems to be confined to times of his dry-land journeys; once in his native element he is again the peaceable, timid animal we know.

The muskrat does not live entirely on vegetable matter. Being an expert diver he does not dive for nothing. He knows just where the clams are lurking in the mud at the bottom. When one of these tight-mouthed morsels is secured the problem is to get it open. But the wily muskrat does not try to pry it open. I doubt if any animal can do that. Even the wise old crow gives up and flies aloft with the clam to drop it upon the rocks below where it breaks open. The muskrat solves the problem more scientifically. He simply nibbles off the hinge of the clam-shell and the two shells separate. No door is any use without a hinge. The muskrat has no key so he just removes the hinge. And the great pile of loose clam-shells to be found near any muskrat hole shows how successful the trick is.

This little furry dweller of the ponds seems to be most at peace with the world when feeding. I have already told how I watched him at his Christmas dinner. There is another little scene which lingers in my memory. We were once out in a canoe on a small reedy lake. Some distance off we saw a muskrat feeding on a raft of floating reeds. Turning our canoe we allowed the gentle breeze to waft us down the lake in his direction. So slowly and silently did we approach that we passed within a couple of yards of the prettiest brown muskrat I believe I ever saw. He was sitting on his haunches eating food from his forepaws as a squirrel would. We could see his little beady eyes watching us as we passed. I suppose he thought we were only a drifting log. So we let him think so and, silently as a drifting log, we passed by leaving him eating in peace.

Winter night ramble
Winter birds

JUST after the first fall of snow one year I spent a week-end in a rough unsettled part of the county near my home. As usual I put in much of my time on Saturday afternoon rambling through the woods and thickets. Early winter is not the best time for nature study. Birds are as a rule few, so that I saw only what I expected of these and a couple of rabbits and one snickering red squirrel.

But on the light snow there were abundant signs of life in the numerous tracks everywhere. From chink to crevice ran the traceries of tiny mouse tracks. The squirrels left signs of their dashes from tree to tree. At one place I found traces of a fox who had sauntered along, leaving his doggy trail. But by far the most conspicuous of all were the scores of rabbit tracks to be seen everywhere. In these I could see that both the snowshoe and the cottontail rabbits had hopped about freely. Along and under the logs, beneath the bushy tangles, in and out about the trees and by the edges of the clearings, their wandering had led. They must often have seen one another, these two neighbours

of the woods, for their paths frequently crossed.

Do you know the difference between the snowshoe and the cottontail rabbits? Few people know there are two kinds in the woods. The snowshoe is the larger animal. His fur is brown in summer and turns white in winter. Wise nature knows how best to protect him in giving him these concealing garments. It is his huge furry paws which have given him his popular name; by their aid, he can snowshoe on the tops of the snow-drifts. The smaller cottontail is more a haunter of the swamps and thickets. Unlike his cousin he keeps his brown coat throughout the year, and his paws are not so heavily padded. Perhaps he does not need snowshoes in his thicket home. Often the only glimpse we see of him is a scared little bunny running at top speed with his cotton-white tail bobbing behind him. But why does not the cottontail change his coat with the seasons, as does the snowshoe rabbit? We don't know. It may be that he finds concealment enough in the thickets. Or, it may be some other very much deeper reason which goes away back in his family history, of which we know nothing. Or, perhaps—oh, there are so many things that might be the reason. We have much to learn yet, even about rabbits.

Seeing as many tracks as I did one would naturally think that these furry little ramblers must be plentiful. But, remember, one rabbit can make many, many tracks. All through the afternoon I actually saw only two of the animals—one·scurrying cotton-tail and a snowshoe which hopped leisurely by. Of course I have no idea how many shy little watchers saw me from their hiding-places. Then I thought: "Perhaps much of this rambling is carried on at night while we humans sleep. During the day the timid little creatures lie hidden in the shrubbery. Tonight in the gloom will be my opportunity to pry into these secrets."

So, after our evening meal, I stole out of the cabin where we were staying, leaving my companion to his book. I wanted to see a bit of the bunny's life when he thought no one was watching. It was a beautiful calm winter night. The sky was clear with an almost full moon which shed a pale light over all the snowy ground. No breeze stirred the air and utter silence reigned, so typical of winter nights, save for the distant barking of a farmer's dog. I chose a strategic spot where I could see a good stretch of white snow, a few raspberry tangles, a few thickets and the dense dark swamp beyond.

It is said that the silent watcher sees the most in the woods. But tonight, though I kept silent for a long time, I saw nothing—nothing but the moonlit snow and its fantastic shadows. I became chilly watching and waiting thus, but one must bear some discomforts to learn the secrets of nature. I thought of many other long silent tense watchings I had suffered to discover something. Surely this was to be one of the loneliest. For aught I knew I was miles from any living creature. Vast space above, all about the dim white ground, and silence. Even the moon, that lifeless orb, illuminating the scene, added a spectral atmosphere to all.

Then suddenly I became aware that I was not alone. Only once before do I recall the same uncanny feeling of there being all at once a living presence near me amid solitude. That was one winter night when, crossing a wide field miles from any living thing as I thought, I saw on the clear moonlit snow before me the tiny shadowy form of a horned lark that I had evidently scared from sleep, running over the snow ahead of me. Now, tonight, as then, nature was adding a little touch of life besides myself to the solitude of the scene. Some distance away I saw the vague suggestion of a movement. So faint was it that I could not be sure of anything. I watched intently in the uncertain light. Yes. It moved again. On came the little apparition nearer and nearer, pausing and advancing, lost to view, then in sight again. At last I could see by its hopping movements that it was a cottontail rabbit. Now, I am going to see something not meant for human eyes, I thought.

The little night prowler hopped timidly across the small clearing and examined a tuft of dead grass above the snow. Then he went to a bundle of long trailing raspberry bushes and nosed these up and down, one after another, as he nibbled the buds off. Under the prickly stalks he went and spent some time amid the tangle, where I could scarcely see his form. At length he reappeared on the clear snow and deliberately hopped to a small sapling, where standing high upon his haunches, he rubbed his chin far up the slim trunk, a delightful stretch and scratch, I thought. Another little tangle attracted him and he gave it some attention.

Then, a long still pause. Had he seen an owl slip by overhead, or a hunting weasel tripping over the snow? Or had he heard a warning sound? Whatever it was he knew he must keep still, for it is the moving object that catches the enemy's eye. I, too, was playing the same game. This trick of remaining perfectly still is spoken of by hunters as "freezing." Tonight both of us were freezing, but I can quite believe that his freezing was cosy while mine was more literal. Yet had I moved he would instantly have seen me.

The danger passed—if danger it was—leaving the little rambler free to hop about once more. Across the snow he came, pausing here and there to nibble, to smell or to listen. He was now but a few yards from me. I could see his actions more and more clearly as he approached; sometimes he sat erect on his haunches, again he crouched low, a tight hump of brown fur. I could see his great ears held up to catch sounds I did not hear, or laid back again to rest.

All at once he became aware, just as I had some time ago, that *he* was not alone. He stopped short, gazed straight in my direction, alert and suspicious. Then like an arrow he dashed off in alarm, in long springing bounds that took him past the raspberry tangles, over the tuft of grass, across the clearing of snow beyond. For a moment I could see his tiny fleeing form growing dimmer and more distant in the pale light, then he was gone.

And thinking to myself what secrets of the woodland folk night hides beneath her sombre curtain, I returned to our cosy cabin where I found my companion still deep in his book.

In the same way as many of our summer birds come northward to us, so our winter birds also move northward and leave us. These latter are only visitors with us during the winter. Their true home is in the far north, that little-known, sparsely-settled region, and there they build their nests and rear their young.

The most typical of our winter birds is the snow bunting. He is a plump little finch, with plumage mostly white, mottled here and there in shades of rich brown, and with black wing-feathers. No bird is more the "spirit of winter" than the snow bunting. He is the true snow bird and is often spoken of poetically as the snowflake. Perhaps this name is suggested by the appearance of a flock of these buntings as they flit overhead, tinkling out their icy notes, their white bodies gleaming in the winter sunshine. One might readily imagine them a living snow-storm borne along on the gale. As early in autumn as October, the snow buntings come down to us from the north, visiting our stubble fields in flocks of hundreds. A weed patch covered in snow, seeming so desolate, is found to be quick with life as these merry little foragers run hither and thither as though enjoying a jolly game of tag to keep warm. In reality they are feeding upon the seeds of the weeds that show above the snow. Scant fare, you think, such tiny seeds in winter weather. Yet every morsel has abundant nourishment, So amid such barren surroundings, these hardy little snow buntings enjoy life and grow fat.

Along with the flocks of cheery snow buntings we find the dainty little redpolls. They lack the picturesque garb of black and white worn by the buntings and are more sparrow-like in their dress of browns and greys. Yet as though to be distinctive, the redpolls wear a jaunty little cap of carmine red—hence their name; and many of them have their breasts suffused with delicate pink.

While the snow buntings are essentially ground birds, walking as they forage about on the snow, their companions the redpolls prefer to perch upon the weeds above the snow and pick the seeds direct from the plant. It seems as if there is an arrangement between the two birds, just as one schoolboy climbs the apple-tree to shake down the fruit for his chum to gather off the ground. Naturally the lighter and better climber goes aloft. The redpolls are small perching birds better fitted to cling to the frail weeds which would not hold the heavier buntings.

The winter woods offer much more shelter and food than the wind-swept fields. There are many kinds of wild fruits which remain on the trees and bushes over winter. The seeds of these provide plenty of food for the woodland finches. Nature has equipped these birds with stout conical bills, by which frozen fruits can be crushed and tough pods broken open to secure the seeds within. The pine grosbeak, the evening grosbeak, the purple finch and the crossbill are all stout-billed birds able to glean their food thus. And what food do they find? The mountain ash, the Manitoba maple, the Virginia creeper, the climbing bittersweet, the sumach and the snowberry and a score of others all display their stores in plain view and some in bright colours as though to cry out, "See, here is food." It is no rare thing for the bird student to come upon a flock of grosbeaks or purple finches in the winter woods all feeding in one tree laden with such fruit.

There are other trees which do not display their spoils in open view. Cone-bearing trees as the pine, the spruce, the hemlock and the balsam, hide their seeds deep out of sight under the scales of the cones. The grosbeaks and finches do not seem to have learned this secret. Even had they, I doubt if they could get at the seeds.

So the harvest is left for the crossbills. It is quite amusing to watch these little parrot-like birds, clinging in the oddest attitudes to the twigs and cones, thrusting their snipper-like bills deep between the scales of the cones and pulling out the seeds. How they tumble about, this way and that, sometimes hanging upside-down, reaching out far to the right and to the left in their efforts to clutch a cone! Then suddenly, in the midst of the banquet, as one bird the whole flock is off to parts unknown, and the tree is left silent and deserted.

So much for the seed-eaters. There are also insect-eating birds which winter with us. The active downy and the robust hairy woodpeckers, the patient little brown creeper and the sociable chickadee all make the woodlands interesting when bird life is at its lowest ebb. Up and down the tree-trunks and among the leafless branches they travel in search of their insect food. We might wonder what insects they could find at this season. Hidden in the crevices of the bark is a juicy cocoon, a nest of spider's eggs or an insect in its deep winter sleep. Other insects boring in the wood or under the bark are pecked out by the busy woodpeckers. Each bird well knows where to search for its food and nature has provided the means for securing it.

These smaller birds are in turn the prey of the larger ones which winter with us. By day the goshawk, the rough-legged and the sparrow hawk can be seen hunting in the woods and fields. And by night the great horned, the barred and the screech owls come forth from their retreats in the thick evergreens to hunt during the hours of darkness for their prey of smaller birds and mice. These are but a few of our winter birds. Hard as their lot may appear to us, and scanty as their fare may seem, they live and thrive. Dreary winter is their season of sojourn with us and it has no terrors of cold or famine for them.

But why should these birds be our guests during winter only, leaving us when there is a promise of better days? Perhaps there is deep in the inner being of each of these hardy travellers that same restless spirit which has ever prompted men to leave home and fireside, to face dangers unknown in far-off lands. The same urge that moved the Spanish to quit their sunny clime of gardens to explore the steaming marshes of America, the venturous Danes to seek out and find the bleak island of Iceland, and the French to venture across the wide uncharted Atlantic to colonize Canada three centuries ago. Our race has ever felt the urge to wander, for far fields ever appear greener.

So, as the sun waxes warmer, the snows of winter vanish, the earth softens and the earliest buds are swelling, these birds of winter wing their ways back again to the north, some going farther than any human settlement; and there, amid the peace and solitude of that great lone yet friendly land, which is really their home, they build their nests and rear their young.

The wood lot

Ramble fifteen

As a boy I recall reading passages in Parkman's works in which he describes this land of ours as it was in the days when the French and English struggled here for mastery. He refers to it all as a great unspoilt natural wilderness of league upon league of verdant forest, stretching far away into the dim hazy distance, unbroken save for here and there a blue lake or a winding river. And he describes the wild life of all kinds to be found in teeming abundance, living everywhere in this vast natural sanctuary undisturbed by man.

What schoolboy has not been thrilled by such a picture, regretting that he was born so late, and that those wonderful days are no more? But, of course, such days could not continue. With the ever advancing tide of civilization, the forest had to go and its wild life with it. It required not only game but tilled fields and crops to feed the stream of humanity from the old land pouring into this new country.

Yet we see with us today, here and there throughout the land, remnants that recall those days of primeval forest. A familiar sight on the landscape is the wood lot, standing out fresh and green with its trees, large and small, and its dense tangle of shrubbery and undergrowth. There are the oak, the birch, the beech and the maple; the pine, the cedar and the hemlock growing just as they did in the days of the French régime on this continent. And not only the forest but in many cases the same wild life finds its home in the wood lot of today.

But there are wood lots and wood lots; those which are left as nature would have them, and those as man would abuse them. I suppose all of us have seen as we have gone through the country the neglected, unkempt field dotted with old decaying stumps and set with a few spindly trees. There is no undergrowth beneath the trees, not even grass. The whole ground is trampled to bare earth and such seedlings as might sprout from the harvest of seeds shed by the remaining trees are trodden down by pasturing animals. Every year a few more of the trees are cut down for firewood. Altogether the wood lot is a pitiful sight and its days are numbered.

But I have in mind another spot. For years it has been my joy to go there. No cattle tear at the newly growing twigs, or trample the forest floor into mud. No careless axe creates devastation.

Amid the shade of over-arching branches there is a cool retreat, and the secrets of the woods lurk on every side.

It is interesting to follow a year through in such a sanctuary. Each season brings its changes in the plant life and the animal world, so that the scenery and the life from month to month is never quite the same. All is a living, changing drama, a fascinating story for those who would read it.

Winter is the season when Nature rests; but even in this, the deadest of seasons, there is much to be seen and much astir that is not seen. Nature reveals her secrets in a unique way. The snow covering the ground smooth and unmarked one day, may, on the next, be a fund of information. Every four-foot which has ventured abroad during the night, every bird which hopped about during the day has left a clear record of its movements. Even the crisp dead leaf blown casually across the snow has left its mark in fantastic scrawls.

The red squirrel has been about. You can easily tell his tracks, for he seldom goes far from the trees. His nervous, active nature is shown in the quick dashes from tree to tree. He is a climber and does not care to stray far from the friendly branches where he is at home. And here is the cottontail rabbit's track. Tall trees mean nothing to him. He could not climb no matter how hard he was pressed. Thickets are his refuge. So we find the marks of his large padded feet winding about, pausing here and there to browse upon the twigs, and finally disappearing into the depths of the thicket.

The delicate bit of tracery along the fallen log shows that a mouse has been abroad. And farther on is a huge gaping hole into which goes the regular four-footed trail of a skunk. He must be still at home, for there is no trail showing he has come out again. What life there is about, even in silent winter! Yet we have not seen a single one of these ramblers. The snow record has told us all.

But we do see other life. There are several birds about. A flock of pine grosbeaks is feeding in the mountain ash tree. The frozen berries are their food. As we watch them we hear low, soft conversational notes expressive of contentment even with such humble fare. Perhaps some bright male gives us a few bars of his song. Thin icy notes, but later, in spring in his northern home, he will sing a richer, fuller song.

The busy little downy woodpecker is here. He knows well how to take care of himself in winter. All day he searches the woods for his food of insects hiding in the bark and at night he sleeps in a hole in the old beech tree. Like him the little brown creeper toils in his more humble way from tree to tree, searching for food. Here too we find the white-breasted nuthatch. He is a skilful acrobat on tree-trunks. It really does not matter to him how he climbs, up, down or across the bark. Nor is he particular what he eats. Insects in the bark or nuts form his bill-of-fare. Beech-nuts, hazel-nuts and acorns are brought and wedged tight into some crevice in the rough bark and pecked open for their kernels. Among the thickets on the ground there is a flock of tree sparrows and juncos. They will spend the winter foraging upon the seeds of the plants showing above the snow. But with the coming of spring they will travel to the north after singing us a few farewell notes—the tree sparrow a lilting sweet song and the junco a silvery trill.

Almost before we realize it, winter is passed and many of the birds are gone to their northern homes. The snow has melted, leaving the ground bare. No longer can we find the telltale tracks. But sometimes we get a surprise. I recall on an early spring day finding a racoon high up in an old maple sunning himself on a big limb. He had come out of a large hole nearby where no doubt he had a cosy den.

Hosts of birds throng the wood lots each spring. Fresh arrivals come in daily. They are now in their brightest plumage and many are in full song. As the trees are not yet in full leaf we have a splendid opportunity to see them.

The chickadee is the first to attract our notice. He may have been here all winter, but as though he wished us to see him now he calls us with a short little whistle, which has been written, "Sweet sugar"—maple sugar, I suppose. And this reminds us of that curious member of the woodpecker family, the sapsucker. He knows as well as anyone when the sap begins to flow. We find his chisellings on the bark of many trees, where he has caused the sap to flow to quench his thirst. The song sparrow has returned and will remain here all summer. But there are several migrant sparrows, the white-throat, the white-crowned sparrows with their plaintive notes, the fox sparrow with his rollicking song, and shy little Lincoln's sparrow hiding like a mouse. The woods are full of those bright little gems of the forest, the warblers. And near the ground we find the sombre thrushes, the hermit, the olive-backed and the gray-cheeked, pausing here on their way north.

Many spring flowers are now blooming. Red and white trillium, yellow adder's tongue, spring beauty, hepatica and bloodroot, all add to the pleasure of a ramble. An occasional butterfly is flitting about. As the weeks go by the freshness of spring gives away to the fullness of midsummer. The migrant birds have passed on leaving the residents here to nest. Now we hear the flowing warble of the rose-breasted grosbeak, and the deep throaty song of the scarlet tanager. As the season advances the red-eyed vireo and the wood pewee still sing their languid notes seemingly so suited to the heat of summer.

The air is full of insect notes now and many colourful butterflies hover about the flowers. These flowers of summer are of a gaudier hue than the pale delicate tints we saw in early spring. The flowering raspberry is aglow with purple. The orange lily and the turk's cap toss their orange-red in full view to the passing bee. Down by the low damp swamp near the spring the mauve Jo-pye weed and the white boneset are blooming together. And open glades are full of goldenrods and the earlier asters adding their gold and purple to the scene.

These are the more conspicuous flowering plants, those which show their glories in full view to the passing insects, and are known to those who visit the woods in summer. But in hidden places in the out-of-the-way nooks, sometimes almost out of sight, others are in full bloom. One must know the woods to find some of these humbler beauties. The wild ginger hides its madder-brown flowers at the very root of its stem, and tells of its presence by scent alone. The fringed polygala, a delicate little purple flower with tiny wings giving it the appearance of a diminutive aeroplane, blooms under the shade of its own leaves. There are orchids so small and inconspicuous we almost pass them by. And who knows the flowers of the climbing bittersweet, for they are little more than tiny green buds?

Yet here all are growing together, the haughty and the humble, in the cool shade provided by the great over-arching canopy of the forest. It may be hot on the open sun-lit fields laid bare by man, but this fertile wood lot, left natural as it is, becomes a refreshing oasis in a dry and thirsty land.

Summer with its heat passes and the cool days of autumn come, bringing changes and new scenes to the wood lot. Bird music has ceased. The woods seem strangely quiet and still. Yet there is plenty of life. Many of the summer birds are yet with us, and with the shortening days the migrants from the north return. They are south-bound now. The gay little warblers are in more sombre colours. But the sparrows and thrushes are wearing their former plainer plumage. No songs are heard. Save for low call-notes, all are silent. When we recall the chorus of bird song that rang throughout these woods in spring days, how strangely quiet all is now in autumn!

The flowers, too, have ceased to bloom but we still recognize their seed-laden heads and colourful fruit. The scarlet haw, the crimson holly, the orange bittersweet and the red wintergreen, appear everywhere. But there are one or two flowers peculiar to autumn days. The fringed gentian in its rich blue is in full bloom and the witch hazel, that plant of many strange parts, is a mass of gold.

But it is the forest itself which gives us the colours of autumn. It would require millions of flowers of many different kinds and of the brightest hues to produce the effect of colour we see in the October wood lot. The scarlet maples, the purple oaks, the yellow birches and willows all blend to make our October forests the richest colour masses on the landscape.

Would you learn the lessons of nature? Would you pry into her secrets hidden from mortal eyes? Then visit the wood lot. Not the ragged remnant of former days where all natural growth is trampled down, and the few remaining trees serve only to shelter cattle and provide firewood. But the wood lot which has been preserved as nature would have it, a home for wild creatures, with its tall sheltering trees overhead, its bushes and shrubbery below and its forest floor deep with grass and sprinkled with countless flowers. There you will find what in these feverish days man most needs, rest and recreation.

This book has been set in Monotype Bembo.

Bembo is a fount first used by the great Venetian printer-publisher, Aldus Manutius, and designed by his punch-cutter, Francesco Griffo. It is called Bembo because it was first used in a pamphlet written by Pietro Bembo.

The Monotype Corporation's modern version first appeared in 1929.

This book was composed, printed and bound in England by Hazell Watson & Viney Ltd Aylesbury and Slough.

The illustrations are by Geoffrey Goss.

Typography and binding were designed by Arnold Rockman, L.T.D.C.